ARMSTRONG SIDDELEY MOTOR CARS

DAVID WELCH

AMBERLEY

First published 2019

Amberley Publishing
The Hill, Stroud,
Gloucestershire, GL5 4EP

www.amberley-books.com

ISBN: 978 1 4456 8599 1 (print)
ISBN: 978 1 4456 8600 4 (ebook)

British Library Cataloguing in Publication Data.
A catalogue record for this book is available from the British Library.

Typeset in 10pt on 13pt Celeste.
Origination by Amberley Publishing.
Printed in the UK.

Contents

Introduction

Armstrong Siddeley cars were made between 1919 and 1960. In that period the factory made around 84,000 Armstrong Siddeley cars which varied from the most basic air-cooled two-cylinder cars right up to the finest 5-litre luxury grand touring cars and limousines. Sixty years on the cars are becoming less well known. Classic car enthusiasts sometimes recall the marque and know that the cars had unusual gearboxes and a sphinx mascot. The people who regularly recognise Armstrong Siddeleys are the older inhabitants of Coventry, where the cars were made and, of course, the people who often introduce themselves at car shows saying that their father/uncle/grandfather used to own one. The people of Coventry remember Armstrong Siddeley because the factory was well regarded. It was said that if a man completed his apprenticeship there then he could leave the company one day and the next day would be guaranteed a start with any other carmaker.

At that time the factory was known as 'The Siddeley' because it was J. D. Siddeley who ran it. The Siddeley was a large factory because the cars were only one part of the company's output. Since the First World War J. D. Siddeley had been making aircraft and particularly aero engines, as well as his cars, and from then on the aviation side of the business became the biggest and most profitable part of his expanding empire. Building cars next to aeroplane engines reflected well upon the cars 'made to aircraft quality' and they were seen as being a cut above the competition. They were hand built and expensive, so few of those who built them could afford to buy one.

Armstrong Siddeley cars did not suddenly spring into existence under J. D. Siddeley in 1919 as he had been involved in the early car making industry since 1902, and even before then as a tyre manufacturer. The story of Armstrong Siddeley cars is the story of an engineering entrepreneur who skillfully built an empire from next to nothing to a major cornerstone in British industry. J. D. Siddeley was both a hard-nosed business man and a gentleman who inspired great loyalty from his workers, and the cars that they made are a fascinating record of British automotive development.

This book is about the cars and some of the people who drove them. There are other larger tomes that go into great technical detail but this book is designed for anybody wishing to know a little more about the marque and its wide variety of cars, not just dyed-in-the-wool Armstrong Siddeley enthusiasts. Wherever possible previously unseen illustrations have been used. Many of the historic photographs have come from the archives of the Armstrong Siddeley Heritage Trust.

1

From Cyclist to Carmaker

The carmaker in the name Armstrong Siddeley was John Davenport Siddeley. The Armstrong appellation came along as part of a complicated history of takeovers, amalgamations and similar corporate evolutions. Therefore, the name of these cars might colloquially be shortened to Siddeley but to call them Armstrongs is inappropriate.

By the time Armstrong Siddeley Motors came into being J. D. Siddeley was fifty-three years old and had been in the motoring and allied industry for twenty-seven years. He was born in 1866, the son of a successful Manchester businessman who owned a hosiery and glove business which included a factory, a mill and two shops. J. D. Siddeley started working in his father's business where he began to learn about management. His hobby at that time, in common with many other young men, was cycling. It was not long before he stopped working for his father and set up his own bicycle shop. He was an enthusiastic member of the Anfield Cycling Club and soon became involved in organising long-distance record cycling events. Sometimes acting as a pace cyclist or riding ahead to check on food and rest stops, Siddeley also telephoned progress reports to newspapers.

J. D. Siddeley, aged twenty-six in 1892, with his hand on the saddle of a Humber racing bike. (Photo courtesy of Bill Smith and the Siddeley family)

J. D. Siddeley then closed up his shop and moved to bicycle makers Humber & Company, where he was on the books as a draftsman and presumably had a hand in designing the bikes used by their racing team, which he managed.

In 1893 he married Sarah Mabel Goodier of Macclesfield, who was to bear three sons and two daughters. In the same year his management skills were noticed and he accepted a senior post in Belfast, where the Dunlop Pneumatic Tyre Company had set up a new factory in 1890. A year later J. D. Siddeley was back in England with his wife and first son, Cyril, still working for the Dunlop Pneumatic Tyre Company. In 1896 this company became the Dunlop Tyre Company and it was also the year that J. D. Siddeley left the company to start his own tyre making company, the Clipper Pneumatic Tyre Company Ltd, in Fleet Street, Coventry. His timing was ideal; pneumatic bicycle tyres were replacing the old solid tyres that had been used on bicycles, but much more important was the nascent market for motor car tyres. At that time it is estimated that there were only around 100 motor cars in Britain, and many of them were remarkably crude machines that used wooden wheels with either steel or solid rubber tyres, but pneumatic tyres were starting to be used.

J. D. Siddeley must have believed that there was potential in the growing motor vehicle market, despite the venom of the establishment that did not see that the days of equine transport were numbered, and certainly did not appreciate their horses being alarmed by these noisy new machines. Most cars were driven by wealthy owners more as a novelty than a practical means of transport. Cars were unreliable and pneumatic tyres, although giving a more comfortable ride, were prone to endless punctures, often caused by lost horseshoe nails. However, Continental carmakers were in advance of British makers and they were making more reliable and, for a price, much faster vehicles.

It is not known when J. D. Siddeley bought his first car, but by 1898 he had a 5.9 hp Daimler, naturally shod with his own Clipper tyres. He had previously overcome accusations of infringing Dunlop patents by securing the agreement of the Continental Caoutchouc and Gutta-Percha Company to make tyres using their patents. A notable feature on Clipper tyres was the provision of threaded lugs on the tyres which protruded through the wheel rim and were secured with butterfly nuts to prevent the tyres rolling off the wheel rim.

To promote his tyres J. D. Siddeley entered the One Thousand Mile Tour of Britain in 1900 organised by the Automobile Club of Great Britain and Ireland. He was an early member of this club, which later became the Royal Automobile Club, and quickly became a committee member. Many of the members of this exclusive club were titled members of the aristocracy and they were influential in advancing the cause of motoring. J. D. Siddeley, with his experience in organising and managing cycling events, must have been useful to the club, and in turn Siddeley made the acquaintance of many powerful people who were to assist him in years to come. The Honorable John Montague drove a 5.9 hp Daimler fitted with Clipper tyres on the One Thousand Mile Trial, as were the cars of a number of other entrants. J. D. Siddeley won a silver cup for his efforts despite sustaining a few punctures and an unfortunate collision with a horse. The car could be quickly repaired, but the horse could not and joined a list of livestock, mostly poultry and dogs, that perished during the event. According to Bill Smith in his book *Armstrong Siddeley Motors*, Daimler were very quick to provide replacement parts for the damaged Daimler, which suggests that they were anxious to see their car do well, and Bill suggests that J. D. Siddeley in the Daimler was

This 1901 advertisement clearly shows the threaded lugs fitted to attach the tyre to the wheel rim. (Courtesy of 'Grace's Guide to British Industrial History')

almost a 'works entry'. The event received a great deal of press coverage and is regarded as a stepping stone in the acceptance of motor cars on British roads.

The success of the event may also have helped J. D. Siddeley decide on his next career move. His Clipper tyres were praised in the motoring press but he resigned from the company in 1901 and started seeking opportunities in car making. With a group of friends he tried to buy his way onto the board of Daimler cars, without success. They later offered him a directorship but by that time he was starting to produce his own cars and they could not reach a mutually acceptable agreement.

In 1902 J. D. Siddeley started a new company, the Siddeley Autocar Company, and by 1903 was selling cars proudly bearing the company name. These cars were not totally original new cars. The first models were a mixture of imported Peugeot mechanicals clothed in coachwork designed by J. D. Siddeley but made by a contractor, or Wolseley mechanicals and coachwork designed by Siddeley. The Wolseley parts came together in the Maxim factory in Kent. This complex arrangement was largely due to the assistance of the Rothschild banking family. Lionel de Rothschild was a friend of J. D. Siddeley and Lionel's family had a substantial holding in Vickers, Son & Maxim, which in turn owned the Wolseley Tool & Motor Car Company.

J. D. Siddeley soon stopped importing chassis and engines from Peugeot and the range of Siddeleys then available were 6 hp, 12 hp and 24 hp cars, all made to J. D. Siddeley's specifications by Wolseley.

The most famous survivor is a 1904 6 hp Siddeley Autocar registration number C85. This car was exhibited for many years at the Armstrong Siddeley factory in Parkside, Coventry, before being handed to the Rolls-Royce Heritage Trust. The car has taken part in numerous London to Brighton runs and has been fastidiously maintained by generations of Armstrong Siddeley apprentices, and is now maintained by the Rolls-Royce Heritage Trust, many of whose members are ex-Armstrong Siddeley apprentices. It is probably fair to say that this car has the longest factory service history of any Siddeley or Armstrong Siddeley car. Another well-known car is the *Green Goddess*, a two-cylinder 12 hp car made

7

THE LITTLE SIDDELEY CAR
SIDDELEY AUTOCAR CO
1903

This 1903 Siddeley Autocar had a Peugeot chassis and engine clothed in a J. D. Siddeley-designed body. (ASHT)

THE "SIDDELEY" 6-h.p. LIGHT CAR is a handsome and powerful car for two passengers; eminently suitable for run-about purposes or touring.

As a run-about, nothing more convenient or handy could be desired, while, as it allows for the storage of luggage, the "SIDDELEY" LIGHT CAR makes an ideal touring car.

Siddeley Autocars are manufactured exclusively for the Siddeley Autocar Co., to their specification, by the Wolseley Tool and Motor Car Co., Ltd., at Crayford, Kent, twelve miles from London.

WRITE FOR FULL SPECIFICATION.

THE SIDDELEY AUTOCAR CO., 79-80, York St., WESTMINSTER, LONDON, S.W.
Telephone: 1671 Victoria. Telegrams: "Sidleth, London."

Sole Agents for "MULLINERS, Birmingham" Motor Car Body. The New MULLINER Patent Phaeton and other bodies can be seen at York Street. Illustrated Catalogues on application.

This Siddeley Autocar advertisement shows the link with the Wolseley Tool & Motor Car Company in the small print. (Bill Smith collection)

This 6 hp 1904 Siddeley Autocar was owned by Cyril Siddeley and was maintained by Armstrong Siddeley and latterly the Rolls-Royce Heritage Trust. This picture shows it after it was removed from storage at Kenilworth Castle, where it was stored during the Second World War. (ASHT)

The same 6 hp car being maintained by apprentices. This car has a horizontal Wolseley-type engine. (ASHT)

in 1904. It was named *Green Goddess* by the wife of a previous owner in the 1930s and the name has stuck with the car. It used to carry a two-seat body but a later owner, Peter Baxendale, had a four-seat body put on this car, probably in part due to his wish to give his friends a ride during London to Brighton runs. A few years ago the engine block split on one of these runs, but a fellow member of the Armstrong Siddeley Owners Club was able to cast a new one, which was soon fitted – resourceful people these car club members. This car is still actively campaigned by Peter's widow, Wendy Baxendale, and gives honoured friends the annual opportunity to freeze or get soaked, or both, on the way to Brighton in November. There are never any empty seats.

If you happen to live in Gozo, the sister island of Malta, the most famous Siddeley – and come to that the most famous car – on the island is *il Karrozza tan Nar*, or the Car of Fire. This 6 hp car, with unusual three-seat coachwork, was the first car to reach the island, where it was owned by a priest and his three sisters and was given the registration number 1. The unusual nickname for this car was probably caused by a tendency for backfiring spouts of flame accompanied by loud reports, which may have been down to poor fuel

The *Green Goddess*, a 1904 12 hp vertical-engined Siddeley Autocar. Its original two-seat body has now been replaced by this four-seat body.

or poor maintenance, but it terrified the local population and unsettled the horses. The car to this day often sets off a loud explosion when switched off. Malta is not known for good-quality petrol. In the end the priestly brother of the Spiteri sisters persuaded them to stop using the car as it was unbecoming for ladies of their status to make a spectacle of themselves. It was laid to rest in a barn for over sixty years before being discovered in a parlous state in 1968 by Maltese resident and ardent car enthusiast David Arrigo. David wanted to buy the car for restoration but, before he was able to make this purchase, it was spirited away by another enthusiast to the UK for restoration in 1971. After a lengthy and active stay in the UK this car has returned to Malta, now in the ownership of David Arrigo. David exhibits and uses the car in Malta and has also brought it back to the UK for occasional participation in London to Brighton runs.

J. D. Siddeley's cars became very popular, partly through advanced design – he was never too proud to incorporate good design features from other carmakers, partly through extensive advertising and partly by organising special events such as the 5,000-mile trial in January 1905. For this trial J. D. Siddeley subjected one of his 12 hp two-cylinder cars to high mileages every day throughout January and into February, until after thirty-eight days a mileage of 5,000 miles was reached. Pity the two drivers and the independent observer from the Automobile Club of Great Britain and Ireland who put up with thirty-five wet winter days and just three dry days, but the end result must have been everything that Siddeley wanted with no unscheduled stops due to mechanical failure and extensive positive coverage in the motoring press.

Ironically, while Siddeley Autocars prospered, Wolseley cars were in the doldrums. Their cars were starting to be regarded as old fashioned partly because the works manager, Herbert Austin, insisted on making horizontal-engined cars, which he felt were superior to vertical engines, as fitted in the Siddeley cars. In addition Austin ran an expensive programme of producing horizontal-engined racing Wolseleys and they failed to pay for

il Karrozza tan Nar, a 6 hp vertical-engined car Siddeley Autocar bearing the registration number '1' on Gozo. Now owned by David Arrigo, this car, which was once in appalling condition, is now immaculate. (Photo by Mark Arrigo.)

themselves in increased sales of the standard road cars. The owners of Wolseley looked for a solution to their problem and found it was staring them in the face: quite literally, as the London showroom for Wolseley was directly across the road from Siddeley's showroom. With Wolseley starting to suffer while the new young Siddeley Autocars were growing, the answer must have seemed obvious to them. The two companies amalgamated. At a stroke Wolseley had enveloped one of its competitors and the talents of Siddeley could be put to good use for Wolseley. One wonders what incentives were offered to J. D. Siddeley to give up his own company, but it seems likely that money and promises of a high degree of control were involved.

J. D. Siddeley was appointed as sales manager at Wolseley while Austin stayed as production manager. Both of these men were strong characters and did not like to be opposed and a good deal has been written about animosity between the pair. Whatever the truth may have been both men had to bow to the wishes of the board of directors and before long Wolseley was offering both flat-engined cars designed by Austin and vertical-engined cars promoted by Siddeley; indeed initially the vertically engined cars were the same as the last of the Siddeley Autocars that Vickers, Son & Maxim had been building for Siddeley from Wolseley produced parts, just the badge was changed.

A most unusual one-off Siddeley car came into being during this period. J. D. Siddeley was happy to enter his cars into reliability trials and hill climbs, and sometimes drove them himself in such events, but he had never built a racing car. Then Lionel de Rothschild commissioned Siddeley to build a 100 hp racing car to enter the annual Gordon Bennett race. Lionel Rothschild was an enthusiastic driver of large fast cars and, apart from one or two Siddeley Autocars that he owned at that time, he had a 40 hp Mercedes. Perhaps the order for a Siddeley racing car was intended to show Austin that Siddeley was being seen as the key man in the new set-up. Lionel de Rothschild wanted to enter the Gordon Bennett Trophy race driving his own car, although this would have been against his father's wishes, but in the end withdrew his entry as driver as his family entered a period of mourning for a deceased relation. It would not have escaped Austin that the racing cars that he was continually developing were being ignored by Rothschild for a racing car with a large vertical engine. The new Siddeley racer was similar to the racing Napiers of the day with a massive chassis carrying a large upright engine under a bonnet that had the wind-cheating characteristics of a small outhouse. The driver and riding mechanic were perched high up with a large petrol tank resting on the chassis behind them.

The rules of the Gordon Bennett Trophy race specified that each country entering could have a team of up to three cars, and the cars had to be produced by the country that entered them. In Britain's case there were various companies that wanted to enter their own cars and so elimination trials were held on the Isle of Man.

The construction of the Siddeley car was completed shortly before the trials began and there had been no time for high-speed testing before the car was shipped to the Isle of Man, but there was time for drivers to test their cars as they undertook practice runs of the 51-mile circuit. During these high-speed practice runs the Siddeley repeatedly overheated in clouds of steam as the water jacket which surrounded each cylinder cracked and allowed

The 100 hp Siddeley racing car built for the 1905 Gordon Bennett Trophy race. This was the only racing car that J. D. Siddeley ever built. (Photo courtesy of Ian Leighton-Boyce)

the water to escape. Spare cylinders were fitted with the same result and on the evening before the trial it was realised that the moulded links that bridged the gap between the cylinder wall and the water jacket were not allowing for the different expansion of these two surfaces under hard running conditions. The solution to the problem was to cut away most of these bridging links with a hand-held hacksaw blade. Herbert Austin joined in overnight with this painstaking work to get the modification finished and the engine reassembled, and by 06.00 the work was completed. According to Lionel de Rothschild's chauffeur, Martin Harper, writing many years later, Austin was none too pleased at having to spend the night working on the Siddeley engine, but it was made by Wolseley and he felt obliged to uphold the company's good reputation.

The Elimination Trials began at 10.00 and the 100 hp Siddeley was doing well until it crashed out and hit a building, and due to damage sustained it was eliminated. This was the first and last racing car that J. D. Siddeley built. The car was later rebuilt as a slightly more comfortable road car and was used by Lionel de Rothschild on his large estate for a while before disappearing from history. Herbert Austin left the company in 1905, Siddeley became General Manager of Wolseley and Austin went on to set up his own company making cars in his name. It is believed that this was a successful venture.

Over the next four years Wolseley cars were marketed under a variety of names: some were called Wolseleys and some were advertised as Siddeleys made by Wolseley, but most were advertised as Wolseley Siddeleys. In reality they were all Wolseleys and were all built by that company, but the name of Siddeley added a certain cachet as his reputation was riding high, helped in no small way by his mastery of public relations and promotion of the cars that bore his name. Between 1905 and 1909 Wolseley produced a huge range of

The 10,000-mile Wolseley Siddeley, with one unscheduled stop after just over 7,000 miles due to a wheel bearing. In the rear J. D. Siddeley is seated next to the RAC observer wearing a flat cap. (Picture from *The Autocar* courtesy of the Vintage Sports Car Club archive)

A group of pictures taken from a 1908 Woleley Siddeley brochure showing some of the range of cars made by the company at that time: i. 10 hp Siddeley Phaeton with dicky seat; ii. 14 hp Siddeley Phaeton; iii. 40 hp Siddeley Roi des Belges side-entrance Phaeton; iv. 45 hp Siddeley Limousine as supplied to H. M. Queen Alexandra. (Pictures from Chris Allen's collection)

A promotional postcard sent by the Provincial Motor Cab Company in Oxford in 1909 describes the taxi as a luxuriously upholstered 25 hp Siddeley.

different models and a wide range of factory-built bodies added to the diversity. Taxis and buses were built as well as a small number of commercial vans and trucks.

In 1907 a 40 hp car briefly gained the non-stop record by travelling just over 7,000 miles without an involuntary stop, although a few months later this record was doubled by a Rolls-Royce.

Siddeley had managed to sell around 100 of his Siddeley Autocars in 1904, while sales of Wolseley cars were around 500. By 1908, sales for Wolseley exceeded 1,400 cars. Total sales were good, but with the company spread over a number of different sites and with the large array of models available the company was not profitable and annual losses were recorded for each year until 1909, when the accounts went into the black again. The increase in production and sales was partly due to Siddeley's skills, and certainly under his management the company's products soon regained the high reputation for modern design that had begun to be questioned towards the end of Austin's time at the helm, but in reality it was probably the growth of interest in motoring that provided a lot of the increased sales. The reputation for high quality was largely due to the skills of the Wolseley workforce, while the models made and the skill in marketing them reflected Siddeley's input.

2

From Deasy to Armstrong Siddeley and the Sphinx

Having put the company back into profit, John Siddeley promptly left Wolseley and joined the Deasy Motor Car Manufacturing Company in Coventry. The Deasy company had been set up by Captain Henry Hugh Peter Deasy, a retired military officer whose only automobile experience prior to setting himself up as a carmaker was the importation of Rochet Schneider and Martini cars, which he sold from a showroom in London, but he had achieved fame by surveying 40,000 square miles of the Himalayas for which the Royal Geographic Society awarded him a gold medal. To help him with the business of designing and manufacturing cars he had secured the services of Edmund Lewis, who had previously worked for Rover and Daimler. Unfortunately the new company, whose cars could be easily recognised by a clover leaf-shaped radiator surround, which reflected Deasy's Irish heritage, was underfinanced and poorly managed. Expenses were high because the administration offices were in London while the factory was in Coventry. The board had decided that the factory should be visited at least once a month, and in between these visits it seems that the workers had to proceed as they imagined the board would wish. What actually happened was that a poor supply ordering system meant that workers used the materials they had to hand, but were sometimes held up waiting for materials or components that were not in stock. These delays sometimes meant that customers were kept waiting for their new cars.

In 1908 relations between Captain Deasy and the rest of the directors reached such a low ebb that Deasy resigned and left for pastures new. When Siddeley joined the company as a director he had a lot of work to do to improve the parlous state of this company in Parkside, Coventry, in a factory that had been previously used by the Iden Car Company. The reputation of Deasy cars had been good and they were one of the companies that stood out among the myriad of new carmakers that were being set up all over the country. Siddeley promptly set about dealing with the issues affecting Deasy cars to make them reliable and to ensure that new cars were delivered on schedule. Costs were reduced by closing the London administrative offices and establishing an agency there instead. Departments in the factory that were not making a profit were closed down and some assemblies, and even major components were bought in. Thus carriage bodies were bought in, and at times so were the car chassis. The old management had been remote but Siddeley's style was hands on. He insisted that all the mail to the company was brought

This is the car you want:

It is distinctive in appearance and possesses many advantages over other types. The engine, placed in front of the radiator, is easily accessible. The thermo-syphon system of water-cooling is efficient and simple. The petrol tank is high up with a gauge in view of the driver. The rear springs—on the Lanchester system—give perfect comfort and greatly reduce the wear on tyres. It is the

J.D.S. TYPE DEASY

Torpedo Phaeton, a graceful development of the latest style of Touring Car avoiding the box-like appearance too prevalent with this style of body. It is upholstered in best quality leather and equipped with two oil side lamps and tail lamp, horn, valances between frame and side step and front wings, and a complete set of tools, etc. Prices complete :

14-20 h.p. - - - £435
18-28 h.p. - - - £555

The extra cost of double extension Cape Cart Hood and Glass Screen, as illustrated, is £25. Our Catalogue gives full details. Let us send you a copy.

The Deasy Motor Car Manfg.
Company, Limited, Coventry.

London Agency : 27, Long Acre, W.C.

MENTION OF "THE AUTOCAR," WHEN WRITING TO ADVERTISERS, WILL ENSURE PROMPT ATTENTION.

As soon as Deasy started making J. D. Siddeley models they were advertised as J. D. S. Type Deasys, and the older models with the clover-shaped radiator were then referred to as standard models. (Courtesy of Grace's Guide to British Industrial History)

A 1910 Siddeley Type JDS Deasy in Australia. (Photo courtesy of Paul Markham)

to his desk for him to open so that he could get to grips with any problems immediately. He also spent a lot of time on the factory floor and came to know every employee by name. Outside the factory, if he met any of his employees in the street he would doff his hat and greet them by name. This style of management was appreciated by the workforce and inspired loyalty.

Within a month of joining the Deasy Company Siddeley was unanimously voted Managing Director by the board and it is notable that virtually every subject discussed at board meetings after this promotion was minuted as being left to the judgement of J. D. Siddeley.

Siddeley knew how car making worked and previous delays in delivering cars to customers became a thing of the past, with the costs of production also being reduced.

Within a year two new models made to his design were put into production. The new models were known as J. D. S. Type Deasys, and Siddeley made it very clear that these cars were completely new by doing away with the whimsical clover leaf-shaped bonnet, which he replaced with a small angular coffin-shaped engine cover (later the sharp edges of the coffin-type bonnet were rounded to a much more attractive shape) with a large radiator behind the engine and in front of the driver. This was not perhaps the most elegant piece of automotive design, but it was instantly recognizable, and if it looked similar to the bonnet shape used by Renault this was no bad thing as French cars had a good reputation. To start with the new models were sold alongside the existing Deasy cars, now referred to as Standard Type with the implication that the J. D. S. Type Deasys were the top-of-the-range models.

The new J. D. S. Type Deasys for 1910 were a 2.9-litre 14/20 hp and a 4.4 litre 18/28 hp, and to reduce production costs the engines were bought in from White & Poppe, a well-respected Coventry engine maker that supplied engines, as well as gearboxes and carburettors, to many carmakers.

The reputation of Deasy was restored and then enhanced by the addition of Siddeley's initials. In 1911 a smaller model, a 2-litre 12 hp, was introduced, and this car used a chassis bought in from the Rover Company with an Aster engine fitted. Business was good and the workforce was gradually increasing. By now the cars were being marketed

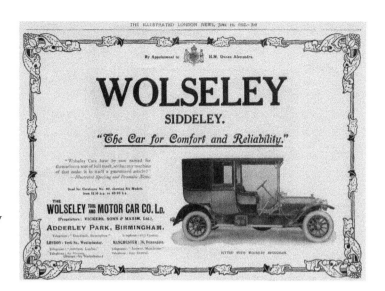

By Appointment to H.M. Queen Alexandra.

WOLSELEY
SIDDELEY.
"The Car for Comfort and Reliability."

"Wolseley Cars have by now earned for themselves a sort of hall mark, so that any machine of that make is in itself a guaranteed article!"
—*Illustrated Sporting and Dramatic News.*

Send for Catalogue No. 40, showing Six Models from 12-16 h.p. to 40-50 h.p.

THE
WOLSELEY TOOL AND MOTOR CAR CO. LD.
(Proprietors) VICKERS, SONS & MAXIM, Ltd.)
ADDERLEY PARK, BIRMINGHAM.

LONDON : York St., Westminster.   MANCHESTER : 76, Deansgate.

FITTED WITH WOLSELEY BROUGHAM

While Siddeley's name came into use for Deasy advertising, Wolseley were still using his name even though he had left that company.

as J. D. Siddeley Deasy cars and this apparently annoyed the Wolseley Tool & Motor Company, which was still using the Siddeley name in its marketing, even though J. D. Siddeley had left that company in 1909. Wolseley insisted that they had sole rights to the use of Siddeley's name and thus the good reputation that customers inferred from it. Although legal proceedings were threatened they never materialised and J. D. Siddeley was able to continue using his name on his cars while Wolseley quietly dropped it from their cars. Common sense had prevailed.

Meanwhile, Siddeley Deasy cars were given a good deal of beneficial publicity from successful participation in the 1911 Prince Henry Auto Tour. The event, instigated by Prince Henry of Prussia, was a friendly, mildly competitive rally, involving German and British teams around a loop in Germany followed by a longer loop around Britain. This event was exclusively for the upper classes of Germany and Britain. Many of the car owners chose to drive their own cars, although usually with a riding mechanic to undertake the greasy bits of maintenance, but some of the entrants chose to use a staff driver. Naturally these drivers and mechanics were not named in reports of the event; indeed, the organisers frowned upon any detailed reporting as they considered it to be a private event, notwithstanding the huge public interest and crowds of spectators lining the route. One driver who was apparently of sufficiently high status to merit naming was George Sharp, an editor of *The Motor*, who piloted a Mr Hasslacher's Deasy. Seven of the British team's twenty-eight cars were listed as Deasys and it is likely that all of these were Siddeley Type Deasys; certainly, a sketch of George Sharp at work on the event shows that he was driving a Siddeley Type Deasy. Overall results were not made public, but to have so many Deasys reflected very well on the marque against the five Daimlers, four Rolls-Royces and sundry other cars in the British team. After the event Mr Hasslacher and John Siddeley presented George Sharp with a commemorative silver clock and in due course this clock was inherited by his son, Selwyn, who became the Publicity Manager at Armstrong Siddeley Motors for many years. The clock is now on display at the J. D. Siddeley exhibition in the gatehouse at Kenilworth Castle.

A Siddeley Deasy with coachwork by Connaught.

A gathering of Siddeley Deasys in the Lake District, possibly for dealers and potential customers. J. D. Siddeley is leaning against the rear wing of the car on the right-hand side. (ASHT)

In 1911 the range of cars had expanded to four models: 12 hp, 14/20 hp, 18/24 hp and 24/30 hp. The latter three were available in various chassis lengths and could be specified with a variety of different coach-built bodies, or new owners could purchase just a chassis and then have a coachbuilder of their choice build coachwork to any design they wished. The same range of cars continued into 1912 but by the end of the year the White & Poppe engine had been replaced by quieter Knight double sleeve valve engines, which further enhanced the perception of quality. At the time a motoring writer is reputed to have described a Knight-engined Siddeley Type Deasy as being 'as quiet and inscrutable as the sphinx'. At a time when the country was fascinated by Egyptology, particularly the pyramids and the mighty sphinx, this phrase appealed to John Siddeley and he adopted the sphinx as the mascot for the company's cars and later the trademark of Armstrong Siddeley Motors. The sphinx mascot appeared on every Armstrong Siddeley car throughout the lifetime of the marque. It started off sitting up on its haunches, before later sitting down in a prone position. After the Second World War it went through more radical changes before returning to the prone sitting position on the bonnet of the final model.

Silence and inscrutability was somewhat tested in 1912 when John Siddeley's long-time friend and mentor Lionel de Rothschild decided upon a brand-new 18/24 hp Siddeley Type Deasy laundelette to use during his honeymoon. According to the report of Rothschild's chauffeur, Lionel Harper, he lost control of the steering when a forged drop arm broke and the car then hit the kerb and slowly turned onto its side. Fortunately the bride and groom were unhurt and continued their journey to Rome while the car was returned by rail to John Siddeley. Also fortunately, Harper had taken a photograph of the broken part, which showed that the drop arm was cracked before the accident. This probably saved him from accusations of driver error and Siddeley was left with the unenviable task of explaining to Rothschild how a substandard part was fitted to the car.

While Siddeley's cars were selling well to the upper echelons of society, he wished to extend his sales to those of more modest means by producing a smaller and lower-priced car, but without affecting the image of his luxury cars. To this end he started selling a 13.9 hp car under the name of Stoneleigh. This car was in fact a Daimler-built BSA design, badge engineered with a new radiator and bonnet, but no sphinx.

A year later the range of cars continued much as before but now they were properly known as Siddeley-Deasys, as the name of the company changed from The Deasy Motor Car Manufacturing Company Ltd to the Siddeley-Deasy Motor Car Company Ltd. The inclusion of Siddeley's name in the company was recognition of the work that he had put in to turn the company around from a failing to a thriving and well-respected carmaker. It is less clear why Deasy's name was retained; perhaps it was to reassure customers that the company remained unchanged in essence, or it might have been at the insistence of the other company directors.

Another big change in the company was a plan to stop using bought-in engines and start making its own. In the event it took longer than Siddeley had envisaged to design and develop new engines, but an 18 hp engine entered production and work commenced on a six-cylinder 30 hp engine. To gain complete control of its production the company also purchased the Burlington Carriage Company, which was based in London and had been

This 1914 advertisement for Siddeley Deasy cars concentrates on the luxury of the make and the distinguishing feature of the coffin-shaped bonnet. The coachwork is less important as customers were quite likely to specify their own requirements.

Car Luxury

THE best definition of Car Luxury is found in the following extract from a letter to "The Autocar" by Mr. S. F. Edge: "A car of great refinement, luxury, and comfort, most pleasing to look upon, extremely comfortable, and absolutely free from rattles or knocks."
This was Mr. Edge's description of a 6-cylinder 30-36 h.p. SID-DELEY-DEASY after he had driven the car over 3,000 miles.

Siddeley=Deasy

MOTOR CAR CO., LTD., COVENTRY.
London Service Depot and Export Offices: Manchester Service Depot: Gt. Northern

One of many 18 hp chassis that were fitted with a standard ambulance body during the First World War. They were often used very close to the front line.

supplying car bodies for the range of factory-built cars that were not supplied to customers in chassis form. Burlington was moved to Parkside and became the in-house coachbuilder. Finally a Stoneleigh light commercial vehicle of 35 cwt had been introduced, although sales of it and its light car sibling were poor.

By the start of 1914 the company had expanded in manpower from around 140 staff, when Siddeley took over, to more than 500 staff. Turnover was growing, especially for the larger cars, and the future looked to be set fair. When war was declared in August of that year John Siddeley accepted the widely held view that it would all be over by Christmas and to hasten this end he told his workers that he expected those men of fighting age to join up and that the company would cease production until they returned. It rapidly became evident that this course of action did not meet the country's needs when, a fortnight later, he received orders from Russia for 200 Stoneleigh lorries, and orders for a fleet of 18 hp chassis to be built up as ambulances. Other 18 hp cars were ordered as staff cars for the army.

Messages were sent to members of staff who had left to join up to return to the factory as soon as possible. For some it was too late, they had already enlisted, so the company was obliged to take on new staff and add a night shift in an effort to meet production deadlines. Experienced hands worked very long hours training and overseeing the work of new staff, and the surge of new orders did not let up. In the book *The Evening and the Morning,* there are reports of employees sometimes working 95 to 110 hours a week, and of some not going home for a fortnight.

During the course of the war Siddeley-Deasy accepted work for aircraft and aircraft engine production on a massive scale. As further orders came in John Siddeley acquired more and more land at Parkside so that the factory could grow to complete its orders. When it did not have sufficient capacity it subcontracted work to other firms, and likewise it undertook contract work to help out other companies where possible.

The welfare of Siddeley's workers who had enlisted or been called up for military service was not forgotten, with regular gifts of cigarettes and cash being sent to those serving at the front, while at home the Welfare Fund assisted those who had returned injured and the widows of those men who never returned.

Cyril Siddeley and other Siddeley family members at the wheel of an 18 hp Siddeley Deasy. This photograph is believed to date from *c.* 1915 and shows a later and more rounded version of the Siddeley Deasy bonnet. (ASHT)

By the end of the war the company had expanded nearly tenfold and apart from a workforce now approaching 5,000, a further 2,400 staff of subcontractors were engaged on Siddeley-Deasy work. In addition the company had achieved a very good reputation for the excellence of its work developing and manufacturing aircraft engines. The company had also made a large profit and the major shareholders had become wealthy. The profit was so large that the Government requested the return of some of this money, and J. D. Siddeley immediately agreed to this. In recognition of those ex-Siddeley-Deasy workers who had fallen during the war J. D. Siddeley had an avenue of trees planted in the Coventry Memorial Park, with one tree for each of the fallen.

During hostilities John Siddeley had realised that when the war came to an end he would need to be prepared to start making cars again for the civilian market, and he was also determined to stay in the aviation business, which was serving him so well; in fact aviation work had become and would remain by far the largest part of the company's work. Making cars stayed close to Siddeley's heart and kept the company name in the public eye, but financially it was a small part of his growing industrial empire.

As part of the preparation for post-war production John Siddeley quietly imported a Marmon car from the USA and had it delivered in 1917. It was stripped down and inspected in great detail as an example of one of the most modern luxury cars available in that country. Many lessons were learned from this exercise, which is a polite way of saying that many good ideas were copied and used in J. D. Siddeley's next car.

In the spring of 1919 Siddeley-Deasy made two announcements, firstly that it had now changed its name to Armstrong Siddeley Motors Ltd, as the result of Siddeley-Deasy having been purchased by the Sir W. G. Armstrong Whitworth Engineering Company. This was a friendly takeover and the new Armstrong Siddeley Motors Company was to take over the aircraft production and business of Armstrong Whitworth. These two companies would both come under the auspices of the Armstrong Whitworth Development Company. In effect this meant that J. D. Siddeley now controlled the Armstrong Whitworth Aircraft Company as well as Armstrong Siddeley Motors Ltd. Although Sir W. G. Armstrong Whitworth Engineering Company were the overall owners, they left Armstrong Siddeley Motors to proceed with minimal interference. It is thought that they were pleased to have divested themselves of the aircraft business, which they probably considered to have a very limited market in peacetime. Under this deal Sir W. G. Armstrong Whitworth Engineering also agreed to stop making Armstrong Whitworth cars.

The second announcement was that Armstrong Siddeley Motors were now selling their first new model – a 30 hp car that was a post-war replacement for the Siddeley-Deasy 30 hp car. This all-new car was a great leap forward for the Coventry factory and bore a lot of similarities with the Marmon 34. The exterior appearance of the new car was very modern for the period and had a distinctive Vee-shaped radiator grille with the top of the grille cowling sloping up to the top of the bonnet. The radiator had moved to the front of the engine bay and the sphinx mascot was now more prominent, being perched on the radiator filler cap. Many would argue that this distinctive front end appearance was at least the equal of the flat-fronted Rolls-Royces or Daimlers. Under the bonnet, a 5-litre straight-six engine had two three-cylinder blocks bolted onto the aluminium crankcase, and the rocker covers were also made of aluminium. The pushrods were located in tubes on the outside of the engine. Many aspects of this design were similar to the design of aero engines, in which its makers were well versed. The chassis used two fairly massive girders, up to 12 inches deep in the middle of the car, and although this chassis was described as lightweight it nevertheless had the capability of carrying heavy formal coachwork if that was what the customer wanted. J. D. Siddeley was pleased with the reception given to the new car and soon sent his second son, Lieutenant Ernest Siddeley, on a lengthy tour of American companies that manufactured cars and car components to see what could be learned that might benefit Armstrong Siddeley designs and production methods. This was a sensible move as while European car making had hardly advanced at all during hostilities, the American car industry had forged ahead.

To facilitate the wide variety of bodies that might be fitted to the 30 hp car by various coachbuilders the suspension was adjustable to ensure that the car would sit level whatever weight it was carrying. The wheels were steel discs which were lighter, more robust and modern in appearance, and were easier to clean than spoked wheels. Electric starting and electric lights were fitted as standard, and from 1922 front wheel brakes were available at extra cost. In 1924 hydraulic shock absorbers were fitted as standard. The range of bodies available from Armstrong Siddeley were mostly made by Burlington, although

This magnificent 1920 30 hp could be described as the model that eventually led to the Siddeley Special Six. Built in the perpendicular style, this open drive limousine requires very tall doors to its motorhome.

some bodies were bought in from other coachbuilders when they were unable to keep up with demand. In addition around one third of all 30 hp cars were sold as chassis complete with bonnet, fixed wings and running boards for customers to take to a wide variety of other coachbuilders. The Armstrong Siddeley 30 hp car was a generation apart from the Siddeley-Deasy cars made before the First World War and customers queued up to buy what the company claimed was the first all-new British car produced after the war. Starved of the opportunity to buy new cars for so long, the aristocracy with old money were joined by the *nouveau riche* in the desire to purchase these expensive cars that most people could only dream of owning. In 1919 the chassis was priced at £660 while complete cars started at £720 and rose according to the coachwork selected. To put these figures into perspective, the cost of the chassis alone would have purchased two average houses in many parts of the country. Although the new model was announced in the early part of 1919, it was to be the end of the year before production was up to speed and the car became available for purchase, after prototypes had been subjected to rigorous and lengthy testing.

In June 1920 Prince Albert, Duke of York, visited Parkside and saw the 30hp car that he had ordered. It was the first of a number of 30 hp and 18 hp cars that he purchased. (*Employees' Quarterly*, courtesy of the Rolls-Royce Heritage Trust.)

This 30 hp shooting brake was ordered by the Duke of York (later King George VI) for grouse shooting at Balmoral in 1928. It now resides in private hands in the USA. (Photo printed by permission of the Sandringham Estate)

One very welcome buyer was HRH Prince Albert, Duke of York, who later became George VI. He was a keen motorist and purchased several of the 30 hp cars, including one which was bodied as a shooting brake for use on the grouse shooting at Balmoral. This car is one of the few surviving 30 hp cars and after spending many years on display at Sandringham it is now in the hands of an Armstrong Siddeley Owners Club member in America.

At the Armstrong Siddeley factory in Parkside, a tremendous amount of work was needed to switch to making these new cars in the space that had been almost entirely devoted to making aircraft engines. It was a difficult period and probably explains why Armstrong Siddeley initially concentrated on just one car model. A second model was introduced in late 1921: an 18 hp 2.4-litre car that was pretty much a slightly scaled down version of the 30 hp car. Almost everything about it was a smaller version of its big sister: the engine was still a bi-block straight six and although a little smaller than the 30 hp car it was still available with a wide variety of coachwork styles. It quickly became almost as popular as the larger car, particularly because it boasted good performance when not encumbered with unduly heavy coachwork, and because its slightly smaller size appealed more to many owner drivers. An advertisement at the time shows the outline of the 18 hp model superimposed upon the 30 hp model. There is not a great deal of difference and a cynic might suggest that the company was illustrating how easily an owner of the new model could be mistaken for the owner of the larger flagship. Whether looking at these cars in the flesh or in pictures it can be difficult for a viewer to identify which model is being viewed if an example of the other model is not present – no chrome badges boasting engine size on the backs of cars in those days. While the 30 hp car's reputation had benefitted from being the chosen car of royalty and other high society figures, the 18 hp model had to make its own way against the competition and a 10,000 mile test around the racing circuit at Brooklands, observed by the RAC, helped to confirm the new model's credentials. The test lasted for twenty-three days, in which the car returned a shade over 24.5 mpg with minimal amounts of oil and water needed along the way. The only involuntary stop that

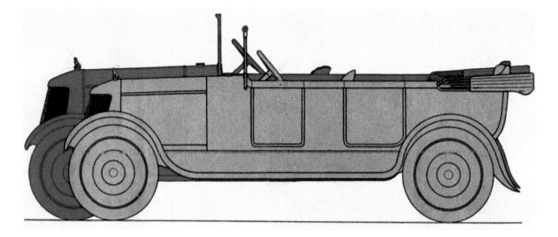

This advertisement clearly shows the similarity in outline appearance of the 30 hp (blue) and newly introduced 18 hp (grey) cars. (Image courtesy of Geoff Elster)

occurred during this test was when a bought-in wheel bearing failed. This test was widely covered in the motoring press.

Although there was an initial surge of car sales as the new models became available, a period of economic depression followed. Armstrong Siddeley was partly cushioned from the effects of this depression by filling relatively small government orders for aero engines, but in April 1922 there was a dispute over proposed wage reductions that resulted in a lock-out until union funds were exhausted and the workforce returned to work on reduced wages.

In 1924 John Siddeley decided to reuse the Stoneleigh brand, which had been dormant for some years, on a new light car to join the increasingly active sector of the market that was being contested by Morris, Rover and Austin, to name but a few. The Stoneleigh light car had a number of novel features: an air-cooled 1-litre Vee-twin 9 hp engine set behind a dummy radiator grille, a three-seat arrangement in early models (one central seat in the front for the driver and two seats behind for passengers), and the absence of a differential. It was not a comfortable car to ride in compared with many of its competitors, although its

One of three surviving Stoneleigh cars. These were lots of fun but very basic compared to an Austin Seven.

The air-cooled Vee-twin 1-litre engine behind the dummy radiator grille of the Stoneleigh. The maximum speed quoted was 42 mph but higher speeds have been reported by courageous drivers.

There is no mention of Armstrong Siddeley on the Stoneleigh car – this car had to sink or swim on its own merits. It floundered and then sank. The tight belt around the badge was perhaps intended to indicate economy.

performance was good. Had it been sold at a very low price it might have succeeded with those desperate to buy a new car, but its initial price was £185 and this cost was difficult to reconcile against the new Austin Seven, which was priced at £165, and was a much more refined car – essentially a larger car scaled down with a four-cylinder water-cooled engine, offering a comparatively comfortable ride and seating for four. Naturally the Stoneleigh did not qualify for the Armstrong Siddeley sphinx mascot; indeed, most people in the factory probably wished that it had never been conceived. A mocking poem about the Stoneleigh was published in the staff magazine and the workers commonly referred to it as the car that made walking a pleasure. Despite a successful publicity gimmick when a Stoneleigh was driven to the top of Mount Snowdon, and a class win in the Scottish Six Day Trial, sales were pitiful. A van version was also a failure and after around 364 total sales the Stoneleigh was quietly dropped. There are just three known survivors, two in the United Kingdom and one in Holland. The two British cars are roadworthy, with one still being actively campaigned by its enthusiastic owner.

Even while the Stoneleigh was proving to be a failure J. D. Siddeley was planning his next new model – a 14 hp Armstrong Siddeley with a monobloc four-cylinder engine of 1.85 litres. It was badged as an Armstrong Siddeley with its sphinx denoting the car's maker visible for all to see, but there was a subtle separation from its larger siblings in its flat radiator. It has been suggested that the flat radiator was fitted because it was cheaper to produce, but surely a V-shaped radiator grille could have been added very easily. The fact that this step was not taken seems to indicate that this car was of Armstrong Siddeley quality but not to be confused with its larger and more expensive models. The first 500 examples of this new model were produced in 1923 and it quickly became a popular car. The build quality was the equal of the larger models yet the price was competitive with other cars of similar size. Performance was sedate but the car appealed to many of the middle classes who aspired to the Armstrong Siddeley name, and it sold well with sales figures barely affected when Morris slashed the price their car of similar size by nearly 50 per cent. Over the seven years it was in production over 14,000 14 hp cars were sold, considerably in excess of the sales of either of the 18 hp or the 30 hp models. Just as with its larger siblings, the 14 hp was available with a choice of body styles, although for obvious reasons a limousine body was excluded from this much smaller car. The car could be bought as a chassis only for coachwork to be fitted by other makers, but this option was less commonly taken up for the smaller car.

In its first form the 14 hp had only had rear wheel brakes, but this was changed to four-wheel braking in 1925 when the Mark Two was introduced, along with a longer chassis and improved suspension. Even with its gentle performance giving a maximum speed in the region of 50 mph, which was considered perfectly respectable at the time, the car was capable of long journeys at near maximum speed. In addition, its tough construction found appreciative buyers in British colonies where road conditions were often poor.

In an unusual promotional exercise in around 1926 three of the 14 hp cars fitted with Sandown bodies and patriotically painted in red white and blue, named respectively as Saint George, Saint David and Saint Andrew, were taken on tour to many towns throughout Britain. The idea was to demonstrate the slow running capabilities of this model in top gear, and where possible these visits coincided with local carnivals to ensure plenty of spectators. Nowadays it may seem strange to accentuate slow running in top gear, but at that time all cars, including Armstrong Siddeleys, had 'crash' gearboxes that called for

The chauffeur driving this 30 hp car is Will Warner and the car was part of a fleet owned by Harrods. (Photo from the collection of Roger Haines, a nephew of the chauffeur)

A section from a November 1925 advertisement for the Armstrong Siddeley 30 hp car. The ruin in the background is Kenilworth Castle, which J. D. Siddeley subsequently purchased and later gave to the nation. It is now in the hands of English Heritage.

1925 14 hp Cotswold Tourer.

a degree of skill when changing gear if embarrassing grating noises were to be avoided. Double declutching is almost a lost art in the twenty-first century but the act of matching engine speed to gear speed was the only way to effect a silent gear change. Apart from nasty grating noises, poor gear changes were often uncomfortably jerky for the car's occupants and could bring a car to a halt on inclines, which then called for a dreaded hill start. Many drivers found this process difficult, especially if they did not drive their car frequently. Thus the ability to run slowly in top gear and to then be able to accelerate smoothly away was a considerable virtue.

A year after the Mark Two 14 hp car was introduced, the 18 hp car was also revised and a Mark Two version replaced the original model. The most obvious change was the engine, which was enlarged to 2.9 litres and was now a monobloc straight six with all its workings contained within the block. It looked neater and various internal modifications gave an enhanced performance. It was a completely new engine, much easier to maintain and had longer service intervals. It was also quieter and smoother running than the engine it replaced. By 1926 the car was available in three chassis lengths, and reflecting the increased power from the new engine was called the 18/20 hp and later became known as the 20 hp. The range of bodies fitted to the various chassis' was huge and there was an even greater variety of body styles added by outside coachbuilders, and just to increase the general confusion Armstrong Siddeley incorporated a lot of detail modifications to the various chassis with almost every batch that was produced. Surely this one group of cars could fill a book on their own. Various examples were owned by HRH the Duke of York, John Siddeley, Lionel de Rothschild and lords, knights and senior military officers aplenty – while other chassis had ambulance and van bodywork mounted upon them. The new 18/20 hp car also provided a very good alternative to the straight six automobiles that were being imported from various American makers, a point that was made abundantly clear in advertising which proclaimed that, 'You cannot buy a better car', and that the Armstrong Siddeley was, 'All British'.

In 1926 it was the turn of the 30 hp model to evolve into a Mark Two version. The most obvious change was in the straight six engine; again this was now a monobloc although the cylinders were bored in two lines of three. It was not until later that the engine was modified to provide six equidistant cylinders in line. Sales of the 30 hp cars were declining over time but it was the flagship Armstrong Siddeley and with its 5-litre engine was well suited to formal coachwork to compete with other luxury carmakers. It was also considered to be a little less ostentatious than some of its competitors, yet still instantly recognisable with its slightly pointed prow and unique mascot.

By the second half of the 1920s things were going well for Armstrong Siddeley; its car and aero engine sales, not to mention a few military vehicle sales, were satisfactory, as was the progress of Armstrong Whitworth Aircraft in nearby Whitley. However, the national economic situation was not good, exacerbated by the General Strike of 1926. The economic recession affected sales of the more expensive Armstrong Siddeley cars but the more modest models continued to sell well.

THE ARMSTRONG SIDDELEY
SANDOWN SPECIAL TOURER
with the rigid and rattle-proof side panels
in position.

When every car was hand built it was easy to offer a range of styles for each model. This picture shows one of the range available on the 14 hp car *c.* 1928.

3

The Introduction of the Wilson Pre-selector Gearbox

1926 was a busy year for John Siddeley. In 1919 he had gained control of Armstrong Siddeley Motors and Armstrong Whitworth Aircraft, but both companies were still owned by Armstrong Whitworth, a company best known for its heavy engineering, shipbuilding and armaments. Now the parent company was going through a very difficult period and he was concerned that an unreasonable amount of profit from his companies was being diverted to the ailing parent company. In business matters Siddeley was astute, and to put a stop to this situation he managed to get an agreement for an unsecured loan of £1.5 million from his bank (it must have helped that he knew the chairman of the bank) and purchased both of the companies that he controlled. Armstrong urgently needed a large cash injection and accepted the offer and Siddeley's terms that they must refrain from future car and aeroplane manufacture.

There was another milestone in Armstrong Siddeley history in 1926: the meeting of John Siddeley and Walter Wilson, the inventor of the epicyclic or pre-selector gearbox. This gearbox had been evolving for many years in the mind of Wilson and stemmed from the use of epicyclic gears in the first British military tanks. Eventually Wilson had persuaded Vauxhall cars to give his new gearbox consideration and after a demonstration where one of these gearboxes was fitted to a Vauxhall car, that company decided to proceed with making them for its future cars. Before this could happen Vauxhall was taken over by General Motors, who were not interested in the Wilson gearbox. The meeting with Siddeley went well and it was agreed that John Siddeley would set up a new company, Improved Gears Ltd, with himself and Wilson as joint managing directors. Wilson would continue to develop his designs and the company would license use of this new type of gearbox to other car makers. John Siddeley was keen to get this new type of gearbox available for the cars he sold as quickly as possible.

The unique selling point of the pre-selector gearbox was that it completely did away with the difficulties of using a crash box, and its use could be mastered swiftly and easily. In use the driver selected the next gear that he wanted to use, by moving a sliding lever to the appropriate marked gear on a steering wheel-mounted quadrant. At this point nothing happened and the driver could change his mind about his next gear choice if he wished, but when what looked like a normal clutch pedal was depressed and released the gear would change smoothly and without any risk of an embarrassing cacophony ensuing.

The system required no particular skill in use and was a giant leap forwards in car design and usability.

In late 1927 yet another new car was introduced alongside the 14 hp, 18/20 hp and 30 hp cars. It was a 15 hp car fitted with a new 1.9-litre side valve engine. In contrast to the other Armstrong Siddeley models, which used overhead valve engines, the introduction of this side valve engine is difficult to understand and seems to be a retrograde step, but there was a sector of the market that favoured this type of engine and John Siddeley was not one to turn down an opportunity. It was not a very costly exercise to bring this car to the marketplace as initially its chassis was more or less identical to that used on the 14 hp cars and the bodies were interchangeable. From the customer's point of view you could order the well-proven 14 hp with an alternative, slightly larger engine. Performance was much the same as the 14 hp engine with a reputed ability to reach over 60 mph, but this was dependent upon the style and weight of the body fitted. The 15 hp shared the good low speed in top-gear flexibility and hill-climbing ability of the 14 hp car, as well as the flat-fronted radiator. Over the years it was in production various modifications were made to the 15 hp car including the chassis, gear ratios and the lubrication system, and a long chassis version was introduced which allowed for a bigger cabin at the notable expense of performance. One surprising modification occurred in 1929 when the 15 hp was given the Vee radiator style of the more expensive models.

The final new arrival in the model line-up during the 1920s came in 1929 in the form of the 12 hp car – by Armstrong Siddeley standards, almost a miniature car. Power came from a 1.2-litre straight six side valve engine, which has been described as a scaled-down version of the 15 hp engine that was fitted to a scaled-down version of the 15 hp chassis. Some felt that the car was underpowered and in 1930 the engine was enlarged to 1.4 litres with a redesigned head and these changes certainly helped to improve matters when a heavy body was fitted. When a lighter body was used the 12 hp performed as well as competing cars with similar-sized engines and could comfortably carry four occupants at appropriate

The gear change control for the Wilson pre-selector gearbox.

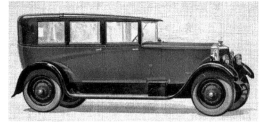

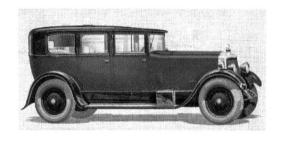

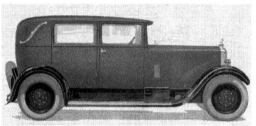

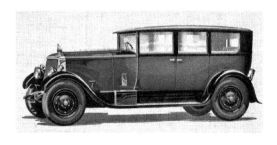

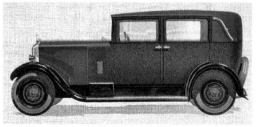

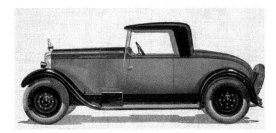
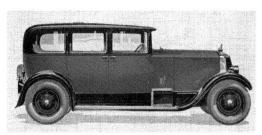

These pictures from a 1928 brochure show more different styles of coachwork over the entire range of different-sized cars. This pocket-sized fifty-five-page brochure must have been prized by any small boys of the era who managed to scrounge one from a dealer or exhibition stand.

speeds on the roads of the day. Dual carriageways were still far in the future and most people in such moderately sized cars were perfectly content to cruise along at 40 mph, although such a speed as an average was certainly attainable if the car was driven briskly. The 15 hp car in both long and short chassis form continued in production until 1934.

By 1928 the pre-selector gearbox was in production and was announced as an option on Armstrong Siddeley cars at an extra price of £50 on the 30 hp car or £35 on the 18 hp model. It was revealed to the public at the Motor Show that year and featured heavily in the company's advertising henceforth. It was described as self-changing and silent, but was usually referred to as the pre-selector gearbox. To describe it as silent was not entirely accurate as it did have a distinctive whine, especially when it was first introduced. Because of the rush to bring the pre-selector gearbox onto the market, the first batches went straight from the drawing board to production. This gave no time for bugs to be ironed out and the factory received many complaints about the excessive noise made by these new gearboxes.

In *Walter Wilson, Portrait of An Inventor*, Gordon Wilson's biography of his father, there is a passage describing J. D. Siddeley's response to these complaints. He recalls how a group of salesmen were invited to Coventry, where they were packed into a convoy of 12 hp cars for a short journey during which the pre-selector gearboxes made all the distinctive whining noises during gear changes that were causing complaints. Afterwards John Siddeley addressed the salesmen, without mentioning these noises, and told them to go away and sell these cars, which he said, 'Any rich man would be proud to give to his daughter.' This exercise put a stop to further complaints, and further refinement of these gearboxes reduced their distinctive sound. Adverts for Armstrong Siddeley cars emphasized that its cars were now easily controlled by women by incorporating illustrations of a female gloved hand on the gear selector and an elegantly shoed female foot upon the floor pedal.

The 12 hp fitted with the pre-select gearbox soon became popular with a significant number of female drivers, who appreciated the Armstrong Siddeley-quality standards that matched the quality of the larger models driven by their husbands or chauffeurs.

The pre-selector gearbox was so successful that it soon became the sole choice on all Armstrong Siddeleys until 1939. After the Second World War the alternative of manual gearboxes with synchromesh was offered, except on the last model, the Star Sapphire, which was only available with automatic transmission.

The pre-selector gearbox was also licensed to various other vehicle makers and was even used on many double-decker buses and most of the pre-Second World War ERA racing cars. When fitted to competition cars the gear selection quadrant is usually removed from the steering wheel and placed in a convenient position on the side of the cockpit. ERA

A 1929 15 hp Open Tourer. (ASHT)

racing drivers valued the pre-selector gearbox because it enabled them to make faster gear changes and due to its rugged reliability, although harsh use in competition called for frequent gearbox rebuilds. One of the most famous racing cars of all time is an ERA known as *Remus*. Its first owner was Prince Bira of Siam (now Thailand) and through various owners since then has been in constant competition use, apart from during the Second World War, and is thought to have been raced more than any other car in the world, with a total of well over 400 races so far – although this number is still climbing as the car continues to be actively campaigned in historic race meetings. The engineer David Morris, who has been looking after the needs of *Remus* and other actively campaigned ERAs for the last twenty-five years, says that its original gearbox was put into its sister car, *Romulus*. *Remus* now uses two gearboxes so that there is always a spare on hand as overzealous gear changing can fill the cockpit with smoke and leave the gearbox in need of a rebuild. The interval between the need for rebuilds can vary between after a single race to after a complete season – it all depends on the skill and driving style of the driver. It is impossible to know exactly how many gearbox rebuilds *Remus* has needed during its illustrious career but David Morris says that it must be in the hundreds.

In normal everyday use in road cars and with normal maintenance the pre-select gearbox is almost always very reliable and trouble free, which is fortunate as rebuilds can be expensive and there are not many people with the knowledge needed to undertake this work.

Remus, still racing after well over 400 races, is seen here at Goodwood.

The cockpit of the ERA known as *Remus*. The pre-selector gear quadrant is mounted on the lower right-hand side of the cockpit.

The habit of constant improvement to Armstrong Siddeley cars, sometimes from batch to batch and sometime as soon as a small detail improvement was conceived, was just about standard practice in the car division of the company. It can largely be put down to John Siddeley's management style, which included spending a good deal of his time on the factory floor. Either he would come up with a new idea or ideas would come from the men who made the cars, which, if considered advantageous, would be added to the cars in production. Although constant improvement was beneficial to owners, it must have been very inconvenient for garages and service agents as they ensured that they had the right parts for any repairs when some of them frequently changed. On the positive side, retrofitting improvements where possible generated extra income. These frequent detail changes are also of interest to twenty-first-century owners of these cars.

At the beginning of the 1930s carmakers were finding that it was no longer sufficient to promote their wares by boasting of high-mileage tests successfully completed without unintended stops, for by this time the reliability of most cars made such exercises much less noteworthy than had been the case a decade before. Sustained high-speed records were of public interest, but they were not the forte of Armstrong Siddeley cars, although record-breaking flights using Armstrong Siddeley aero engines did catch the public imagination and much use was made of them in advertising the 'cars of aircraft quality'. The public now wanted more excitement, especially high speeds, and success on the racetrack was undoubtedly an aid to publicity and sales. Armstrong Siddeley had never built a racing car or competed in any motor racing, and the chance of this ever happening became very remote when John Siddeley was seriously injured in a motor accident which kept him away from work for many weeks. Mr Siddeley was not impressed by sheer performance; his cars were built by craftsmen to be comfortable, reliable, safe, rugged and stylish. After he recuperated from his accident, all Armstrong Siddeley cars were fitted with Triplex safety glass windscreens.

There was however one type of motor sport which did suit Armstrong Siddeley cars and that was long-distance rallies. In that period rallies were for normal factory-made cars and were a tough test of both the cars and their crews. Demanding average speeds had to be maintained from point to point and no time was set aside for maintenance and running repairs. Any time needed for such attention needed to be made up by instantly driving that much faster to avoid being late at the next checkpoint and thus losing points. If rally crews were lucky and the road conditions were easy they might just have time to grab a few hours rest here and there; if not, the only chance of a rest was to sleep in the back of the car while another crew member took over navigating or driving duty. There were no scheduled rest periods in rallies lasting for days, but crews were not limited to two people; indeed, extra points were given to larger crews as their cars were carrying extra weight. Finally there were no service crews; if a car had problems of any sort it was up to the car's occupants to sort them out, either with spares that they carried or with whatever help they could find locally, and all the time the clock was ticking. Such events were a world away from the World Championship Rallies of today.

Armstrong Siddeley Motors entered factory cars, either singularly or in teams, in a number of rallies with considerable success. This may well have been at the initiative of Cyril Siddeley, John Siddeley's oldest son, who was a director of the company. Second son Ernest was also a keen motorist and often took new models on long-distance tests around Europe to ensure that they were up to scratch and to highlight any faults. Cynics might say that the extended tests were just an excuse for a touring holiday, but these intentions were not mutually exclusive.

Although most of the big rally prizes were usually won by powerful sports cars, there was still plenty of kudos to be gained from class wins, team awards and elegance/equipment awards. When weather conditions were bad the speed advantage of the sports cars was negated and rugged reliability and driving skills came to the fore. Another benefit for the factory-entered cars occurred when well-known motoring journalists could be persuaded to drive them as their reports were usually favourable as a consequence – these writers knew which side of their bread was buttered. Savvy readers were able to discern the difference between polite compliments and enthusiastic praise.

By 1931 the old 18 hp model had evolved to such an extent that the new 20 hp, the current step in its evolution, had become almost unrecognisable from its earlier form. It was sleek, stylish and had very good performance for the time. So it was that one of these cars, known as the *Silver Sphinx*, was entered into the 1931 Monte Carlo Rally and driven by Sammy Davis, a famous racing driver (especially for W. O. Bentley) and motoring journalist of the time. Despite adverse conditions the three-man crew managed to outpace more powerful rivals, and after what Sammy Davis reported as one eleven-hour run through France at full throttle, the team was so far in advance of their schedule that they managed to grab four hours of rest in a hotel. One of the team noted, 'It was here that our mechanic was re-introduced, after a lengthy period of happy forgetfulness, to the continental breakfast, a shock from which he never really recovered.' The *Silver Sphinx* was the first car from a European start to reach Monte Carlo, winning first prize, an 'Auto' gold medal, plus the Grand Prix d'Honneur for the magnificence of its coachwork and outstanding condition at the end of the rally.

The *Silver Sphinx's* next task was a tour of British showrooms, where it substantiated one of the company mottoes: 'You cannot buy a better car'.

Further successes followed. In the 1932 RAC Rally, which followed an extensive route around Britain, Armstrong Siddeley cars won three prizes for excellence of coachwork, seven special plaques, two of the principal rally prizes and a special prize for best performance in the over 1,100cc class, the latter probably being won by a 12 hp model. This was the first RAC

The rally success of the *Silver Sphinx* led to this car being named the 20 hp Rally Tourer and a similar body could also be specified on the long 15 hp chassis. (ASHT)

Rally. It featured multiple starts around the UK with all competitors having to complete a course of 1,000 miles before the finish in Torquay. Although the Armstrong Siddeley haul of awards was pretty good (this was confirmed in the company's advertising), there were so many awards that the prize-giving ceremony must have been a marathon itself.

This new rally may not have been the most rigorous rally, especially when compared with the Monte Carlo Rally and the Alpine Rally, but it did have the distinct marketing advantage of getting cars in front of a very large number of British spectators, or potential customers in the eyes of the sales department of Armstrong Siddeley Motors. That said it was still a tough event, run in winter, and not for the faint-hearted.

Another award in 1932 was for John Siddeley; he was awarded a knighthood for services to the mechanical development of the armed services. This honour recognised both the continuing development and manufacture of aero engines and aircraft as well as the work that had been carried out on the development of new military vehicles and the engines to power them.

For 1933 Armstrong Siddeley decided on a much more focused approach to the RAC Rally, but before reporting on that event it is relevant to consider a new car model that was launched by Armstrong Siddeley that year – the Siddeley Special Six. This car was large, luxurious and just the sort of car to compete with the likes of Rolls-Royce and Bentley cars.

The idea behind this large car is reputed to have originated when a Dr Ainscow had the temerity to park his Chrysler outside Crackley Hall, near Coventry, where the Siddeley family were living at the time, when he came to visit one of Sir John's daughters, who he was courting. Foreign cars parked outside the family house did not sit well with Sir John, who was strongly nationalistic when it came to cars, but Dr Ainscow persuaded Sir John to borrow the Chrysler for a few days in return for the loan of an Armstrong Siddeley car during the period. If the legend is true Sir John was greatly impressed by the Chrysler and decided that he would build an equally impressive car. It is a good story and it is widely believed that the impetus behind the introduction of the Siddeley Special Six was to compete with the highest-quality cars in the market. There is probably some truth in the story; Dr Ainscow was certainly real because he went on to marry Nancy Siddeley and their son Derek Ainscow is currently the president of the Armstrong Siddeley Owners Club.

A 1934 12 hp Sports Coupe – and before you ask the red car to the right is a Paramount and has no place this book.

Bodies by outside coachbuilders were less common on the smaller cars, which makes this 12 hp Charlesworth-bodied car a rarity.

4

The End of the J. D. Siddeley Years at Parkside

The Siddeley Special Six was very advanced for the period, but it was also a development of the 30 hp series of models that had been part of Armstrong Siddeley's range for many years. The new car was marketed as the Siddeley Special Six, with the Armstrong part of the maker's name dropped, to differentiate it from the company's other cars and put it in a class apart. These days the term 'special' is usually taken to mean a car that has been modified to change it from original factory specifications, but when J. D. Siddeley called the car 'Special' he meant exceptional.

A lengthy gestation period produced a car that was quite different to its predecessors. It was reputed to be capable of 100 mph, and indeed this might have been true with light and streamlined coachwork fitted, but with formal coachwork fitted the car weighed around 2 tons and to achieve this speed would have been an aspiration rather than a reality. However, performance was very good for such a large car, helped by its 5-litre Hiduminium alloy engine. Hiduminium was a light aluminium alloy that had been developed for use in aircraft engines and it was made by High Duty Alloys – one of Sir John's companies. The same alloy was used for various other components in the Special Six.

The car was launched in 1933 and in 1935 a Mark Two was introduced with various engine modifications and a second SU carburettor that gave a modest increase in performance. The car was also available in short or long wheelbase versions. When production ceased, 253 Special Sixes had been sold, but sadly their survival rate is very low, largely because the Hiduminium alloy, which contributed to the good performance of these cars, was urgently required for the war effort a few years later and the majority of them were scrapped so that the alloy could be recycled for aviation use. After 1945, austerity meant that these thirsty cars – think 6 to 8 miles to the gallon – were not very popular and more were scrapped or dragged into barns to be forgotten. There are now few Siddeley Special Sixes left and probably less than ten that are still roadworthy. It would be good to think that the non-roadworthy cars will be restored to their former glory, but their survival rate in original form has not been helped by the conversion of a few restoration cases into pseudo racing cars. With shortened chassis, lowered suspension and racing-type two-seater bodies and the fitting of large superchargers, they look magnificent but are of limited use; they do not qualify for historic racing championships as they never raced in period, and engaging the blower for more than a few seconds at a time is a great way to start destroying the innards of the engine. Long-stroke engines are not suited to the addition of supercharging

The elegant
simplicity of the
5-litre Hiduminium
engine in
a Siddeley
Special Six.

and the lessons of history show that Henry Birkin's blower Bentleys lacked reliability, although they were good for goading the Mercedes SSK cars they raced against to engage their blowers with crippling results at Le Mans.

The factory offered the Special Six with a variety of different coachwork styles and many Special Sixes were sold as chassis to which other coachbuilders added a wide variety of body styles. Buyers of these cars were predominantly affluent and successful, and perhaps sometimes buyers chose these cars as a more individual, and more modern, alternative to the Rolls-Royce cars that were the traditional choice of the establishment. The slightly pointed radiator grille with its proud sphinx mascot gives the Special Sixes a sleek and more stylish appearance, although the reputation exuded by the Spirit of Ecstasy is difficult to beat.

The Special Six is, with any coachwork, a very large car. For its period it was also a fast car, and it was suggested that either one of them or a small team might be entered into the Le Mans 24-hour race. With a suitable lightweight body, its rugged construction and its pre-select gearbox for rapid gear changes (but not with a supercharger), it may have performed rather well. Probably only Armstrong Siddeley enthusiasts would dare to dream of what just might have happened if Siddeleys competed against Bentleys.

Sir John Siddeley put a stop to any idea of a factory team entering this event, but he did offer W. F. Bradley, a motoring journalist, the use of a Special Six to undertake a survey of the road from London to Istanbul, and back using a different route, for the Automobile Association. This complete journey of over 4,000 miles went rather well. The route included everything from first class roads, which enabled the car to cruise along at 80 mph, to muddy cart tracks and perilous mountain passes which tested the endurance and strength of the car. The run was written up in a complementary article in *The Autocar* which highlighted the only repairs needed on the run were a couple of broken ignition wires that were easily fixed and a broken windscreen wiper that was quickly replaced. This was the sort of positive publicity that Sir John liked and he had the article reprinted so that copies could be given away in showrooms. No mention was made of the amount of fuel consumed en route, which must have been prodigious, but then if you were the sort of person to consider buying a Special Six such considerations were unlikely to be a concern.

A 1934 Siddeley Special Six by Burlington.

A Siddeley Special Sports Saloon. Perhaps 'Sports' is a misnomer in this long wheelbase luxury limousine with a glass partition and fitted cocktail cabinet, but she could certainly show a clean pair of heels to most other cars on the road at the time. (Author)

Exclusive design Vanden Plas Close Coupled Coupé Cabriolet on New Siddeley Special Chassis

The Vanden Plas Close Coupled Coupe Cabriolet on a Siddeley Special Six chassis looks good in this picture...

...and even better in real life. Despite the faux pram irons, only the section of the roof above the front seats opens, which leaves rear-seat passengers in the gloom while the occupants of the front seats have a wonderful view over the long bonnet.

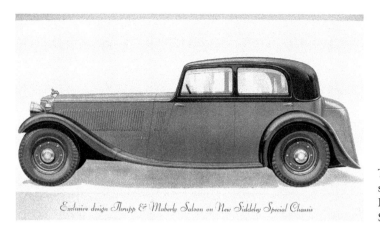

Exclusive design Thrupp & Maberly Saloon on New Siddeley Special Chassis

This brochure picture shows a Thrupp & Maberley Saloon-bodied Siddeley Special Six.

This Siddeley Special Six has a limousine body by Hooper.

FSK 145

This is the front of the Hooper-bodied limousine. The front view of most Siddeley Special Sixes is broadly similar as most coachbuilders retained the factory-style radiator grille and front wings.

This 1936 Siddeley Special Six carries a later and more modern-looking version of the Burlington Sports Saloon coachwork.

Of all the variations of coachwork fitted to the Siddeley Special Six, this streamlined version by coachbuilders Lancefield was the most extreme. It was built for financier George Wansborough who, in later years, helped to finance Gordon Keeble cars. The bodywork on this car had luggage compartments built into the front wings. (Photo courtesy of Andrew Minney)

This Siddeley Special with Vanden Plas Open Tourer coachwork carries Cyril Siddeley's personal number plate, A 52, but it is probably not him and his family in the picture. It was a car with this coachwork, possibly the same car with a different registration number, which Mr Bradley drove from London to Istanbul and back surveying the route for the AA. (ASHT)

Although only 253 Siddeley Special Sixes built over a period of four years hardly rates as an unqualified success, looked at in another way the Special Six was the most splendid evolution of the 30 hp models. The 30 hp was the first car to carry the Armstrong Siddeley name and the final version bore only J. D. Siddeley's name. It embodied all that was best in traditional values as well cutting-edge car technology with the extensive use of Hiduminium alloy for many mechanical and body panels, and of course the pre-selector gearbox. It was probably the one car that summed up all of J. D. Siddeley's aspirations, and was surely the car that he would have liked to be remembered by. His son Cyril Siddeley was a great exponent of the car and entered his own Special Six, bearing the family registration number C52, into a number of rallies as well as using it for everyday transport.

Siddeley Specials were also part of the range of Armstrong Siddeley cars that were entered by the factory in the 1933 RAC Rally. The total group consisted of three Siddeley Specials, a long Twenty Town Brougham, a Sports Twenty Saloon, two long Fifteens, a Twelve Coachbuilt Saloon and an Economy Twelve. This range of cars covered pretty much every class in the rally and must have made a particularly strong impression on spectators at the finish in Hastings as by prior arrangement the whole team had met up outside the town, to be washed and polished, before proceeding in close formation along the front to the finish line. Awards were not so numerous that year but the Siddeley Specials, piloted respectively by S. C. H. Davies, Sports Editor of *The Autocar*, Humphrey Symons of *The Motor* and lastly Cyril Siddeley, attracted a great deal of favourable comment. The Fifteen Sports was driven by Mrs T. H. Wisdom, a well-known race and rally driver, who summed up her impressions in the *Employees' Quarterly*:

It was the first time I had driven a car with self-changing gears and I must say I found it very light and easy to handle. What impressed me first after the ease of control was the super cornering and wonderful stability of the car. The self-centering steering and road holding capabilities of the car are almost up to racing car standards. The self-changing gears made our task very easy and definitely does not take the fun out of driving. We found the body most comfortable especially the rear seat, and by keeping up a good average speed were able to enjoy substantial stops at all the controls. In several cases we arrived before the controls were open.

Naturally the company made good use of all such comments and Mrs Wisdom's words must have appealed to potential female customers, particularly those who liked to drive with a certain verve.

Buoyed by two successful years entering the RAC Rally, the company hit upon a new gimmick to attract attention to the Armstrong Siddeley factory cars in the event in 1934. Nine assorted models were entered, with each painted in a colour of the rainbow. The end of the road section that year was in Bournemouth and it was arranged that the rainbow cars from their various starts around the company should meet up before parading into town in the appropriate order dictated by a rainbow's spectrum. The cars all arrived in time to be cleaned and polished for their parade into town, but the prize tally was disappointing for the Armstrong Siddeleys, with Cyril Siddeley winning a class second prize in his rainbow car. Another rainbow car was awarded a gold medal (among many) for losing no points on the route to Bournemouth. The company was probably anticipating a better haul of awards when they booked space in the motoring magazines with a distinctive rainbow-themed advertisement. This advertisement had an uncharacteristically clumsy tag line: 'We did exactly as intended and rallied where the rainbow ended.' It seems likely that if the results had been better the tag line would probably have mentioned pots of gold at the end of the rainbow and that the large expanse of sky pictured in the advertisement would have been overprinted with details of their various awards.

By 1934 the 15 hp car was phased out and it was replaced by the new 17 hp model. The new car was a logical progression from the older model but the engine was a major step forwards from the old side valve engine. The new engine had overhead valves and the capacity was increased to 2.4 litres and, as with the model it replaced, the 17 hp car was

The procession of Siddeleys entering Hastings at the end of the rally. C52 is Cyril Siddeley's Special Six. (ASHT)

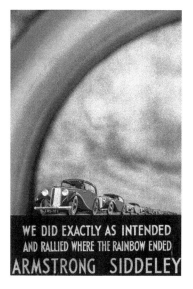

Above left: The full-page 'We did exactly as intended...' advertisement. Plenty of space in the sky but no mention of the small number of awards won.

Above right: One of the 12 hp cars that took part in the Rainbow group in the 1934 RAC Rally, still bearing its original registration number. (Photo by Chris Allen, who owned the car at the time)

available in short and long chassis versions. Another major improvement was incorporated in 1936 with the fitting of a Newton centrifugal clutch. This arrangement made gear changes from the pre-selector gearbox, which could be a bit jerky, much smoother. As ever there was a good choice of body styles available from the company as well as many independent coachbuilders awaiting customers who wished for a variation from the standard offerings.

In 1935 an alternative 12 hp model was made available, known as the Twelve Plus. The chassis dimensions were the same as for the old 12 hp car but it was made to a new and stronger design and was fitted with a new six-cylinder overhead valve engine with an enlarged capacity of 1.7 litres which produced 14 hp. By 1936 this car had changed again with the introduction of a larger chassis but retaining the same engine and the car then became known as the 14 hp model. Despite the confusing nomenclature the Twelve Plus/14 hp cars were popular and performed very well, especially when fitted with the pre-selector gearbox and centrifugal clutch.

The final model in the range to be updated was the 20 hp car. Again, the chassis size was increased, but so was the engine capacity, which was now 3.7 litres, and so the good performance of the earlier 20 hp was retained despite an increase in overall weight. With these and various other revisions the 20 hp became known as the 20/25 hp. The chassis was still available in two lengths and as usual a variety of body styles were available. Many of these cars had particularly attractive coachwork fitted by independent coachbuilders.

The result of these various changes was to produce a range of cars which utilised similar design concepts over a range of sizes: 12 hp, 14 hp, 17 hp, 20/25 hp and the Siddeley Special. Over the years all of these cars, fitted with pre-select gearboxes, had been greatly improved. They all had straight six overhead valve engines and the V-fronted radiator grille

A 1936 12 hp Sports Tourer.

synonymous with the marque. With modern engine and suspension design they were easy cars to drive and comfortable to ride in. Performance had at least kept pace with that of their competitors and the 20/25 hp and Siddeley Specials could show a clean pair of heels to many cars in their class. The only aspect of the cars that had remained constant was quality in engineering standards and overall finish.

In 1935 J. D. Siddeley was approached by Thomas Sopwith, of Sopwith Camel fame, and at that time the chairman of the Hawker Aircraft Company. Terms were agreed and Sir John sold his entire portfolio of companies to Sopwith. Armstrong Siddeley cars were of no great interest to Thomas Sopwith, but Armstrong Siddeley aircraft engines and the other aviation companies such as Armstrong Whitworth Aircraft Ltd, High Duty Alloys (which made light alloys predominantly for aircraft engines) and A. V. Roe, definitely were of interest and were major additions to Sopwith's empire. The actual terms agreed for the takeover are unclear to this day as they are regarded as secret by the Public Records Office and not to be released until 100 years after an investigation into the takeover was completed. In *Pure Luck*, Alan Bramson's biography of Thomas Sopwith, Sopwith is recorded as saying that the day he signed the contract to buy Sir John Siddeley's companies was the scariest day of his life. At that time he did not actually have sufficient funds in place to pay for his purchase, which puts the legality of the takeover in doubt. However, at the time Hawker Aircraft were busily engaged in making three squadrons of Hawker Hurricane aircraft for the Royal Air Force, and were making preparations for the large-scale production of these aircraft. It is significant that Sopwith went ahead with making the aircraft at a time when another war against Germany was expected, but the government had yet to commit to buying these aircraft in large numbers – a bold move that enabled the RAF additional time to re-equip with modern fighter aircraft and to train pilots for the anticipated hostilities. Without this foresight the Battle of Britain may well have ended differently. No doubt all will become clearer when the papers concerning the takeover are made public.

The sale of the Armstrong Siddeley group of companies made the wealthy John Siddeley a very rich man indeed, as his portion of the sale price was thought to be around £1 million. Some people have pondered why he went ahead with the sale rather than keeping ownership within the family. His thoughts on this matter have never been made public, but perhaps he felt that technology, particularly on the aviation side, was proceeding at a pace that was beyond his understanding and that to keep up with such progress more expert leadership was needed. Two of his sons, Cyril and Ernest, held directorships in some of his companies, but like their father neither of them had had a formal technical education. After John Siddeley retired in 1935 he made many generous donations to worthy causes, especially in the Coventry area in recognition of the work of so many Coventry people that had helped him become a success.

A 20/25 hp with cabriolet coachwork by Salmons Tickford. The hood on this opulent car is closed by winding a handle.

This glorious car is a 1937 20/25 hp with a Maltby 'Redfern Tourer Coupe' body. There is a just-visible step on the back of the rear wing to aid access to the folding dicky seat.

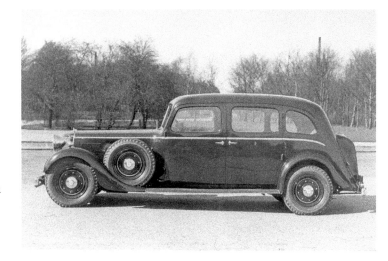

This good-looking 20/25 hp with a body fitted by an unknown coachbuilder was made in 1938 for the Prince of Denmark. (ASHT)

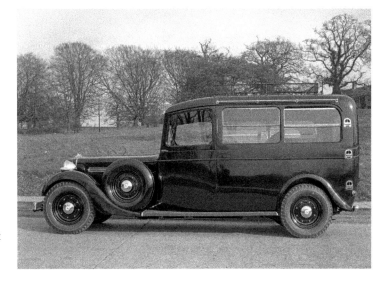

This unique 1938 'mini bus', probably used for transport on the owner's estate, is thought to be on a 20/25 hp chassis. It was built as a one-off for a Mr Phillip Hill. The rear compartment had seating for six people. (ASHT)

A 1937 25 hp limousine. This car is believed to be one that was personally owned by Prime Minister Neville Chamberlain. (ASHT)

5

Thomas Sopwith
Takes Control

Despite the takeover by Thomas Sopwith Armstrong Siddeley Motors carried on in much the same way as before. Sopwith wanted all of his companies to work autonomously, although he did expect them to co-operate to mutual advantage when circumstances permitted. The car division of Armstrong Siddeley Motors, a minor part of the enlarged organisation, was free to carry on as before, and there were no direct competitors within the new group of companies.

The first completely new car to be produced after Lord Kenilworth (Sir John Siddeley was ennobled when he retired and as a baronet chose that title) had sold his companies was an entirely new design of 16 hp. Although it had a traditional straight six engine of 2 litres, the length of the stroke was shorter, pro rata, than other engines produced by the company to give smoother running at higher speeds. This change was appropriate considering the steady improvement of Britain's roads and the increasing performance expectations of motorists. The car, available in just one length of 14 feet 1½ inches, was provided with two optional bodies: the coach saloon or the Four-light Touring saloon. Only around half a dozen of the 961 cars built went to outside coachbuilders. Sales would have been greater but production was curtailed by the Second World War.

Other new cars were being prepared before the war intervened including new versions of the 12 hp, and the 20 hp car which would have been like a big sister for the 16 hp car and used a new 2.8-litre engine. Perhaps the most significant change would have been the addition of Girling independent front suspension. An approach had been made to Mercedes to use their suspension system but this would have been more expensive, and as events turned out would have been seen as unpatriotic. But all this is 'would haves' and 'could haves' because these projects were stopped in early 1940 after just a few prototypes had been built. They were later dismantled and from then on the only cars made were for military use or essential war work.

The new Managing Director of Armstrong Siddeley Motors, Frank Spriggs, was reluctant to go ahead with the new project as it was felt that it would, at best, make only a small profit per car if the example of the 16 hp car was taken as a guide. A rather bigger factor that predicated the end of the 20 hp were unmistakable signs that Britain was almost certainly going to be drawn into another European war. British industry was already starting to prepare for hostilities as massive increases in equipment of all varieties were

The Atalanta, named after the Armstrong Whitworth airliner of the same name. This style was available on both 17 hp and 20/25 hp chassis. The picture here shows the 20/25 hp version, which has a longer bonnet that adds extra elegance. Very few examples remain in existence. (ASHT)

One of the last cars made before the Second World War was this 1939 16 hp Saloon.

Very few of these 20 hp Ensign cars were completed before production was abruptly terminated in favour of preparing for war work. (ASHT)

This picture of a new 12 hp mock-up was taken in April 1940. It was never put into production. (ASHT)

being ordered to modernise and enlarge Britain's Army, Navy and Air Force. New models stood no chance in that climate.

During the Second World War the whole of the Hawker Siddeley group of companies were devoted to military production. Armstrong Siddeley Motors had started producing torpedo engines and gyroscopes well before the war, but this work now escalated, as did the production of aircraft engines. Wilson gearboxes were assembled for Matilda tanks from outsourced parts. Armstrong Whitworth Aircraft produced the Whitley bomber and then the Avro Lancaster that replaced it. Air Service Training, one of Armstrong Siddeley's subsidiary companies, became a centre for aircraft repair and conversion at Hamble on the south coast, while its new training centre at the newly constructed airfield at Ansty just outside Coventry became the production centre for the de Havilland Mosquito. Enemy air raids that devastated the heart of Coventry also wrought extensive damage at the Armstrong Siddeley works in Parkside, but even after the most severe damage production was quickly resumed either in the factory or at alternative sites that could be pressed into use.

Naturally car production was at first severely restricted and then virtually halted during hostilities, although approximately eighty-five cars were built for military and approved wartime work customers. During the war the company was obliged to commit all its efforts to wartime work but, just as John Siddeley had realised two decades earlier, the company needed to be ready for peacetime production as quickly as possible to soften the effects of a sudden dearth of military contracts. Permission was granted for a very few workers to be allocated to work on cars for post-war production, with the proviso that wartime work was not to be affected. A few workers were allocated to this work, much to their initial chagrin as they felt that they were no longer 'doing their bit' for the war effort. Initial design work commenced in 1943 and three prototype chassis were built and fitted with new bodies. The engine used was a development of the pre-war 16 hp engine but the all-new experimental chassis was heavier and more rigid than the pre-war version. Externally the experimental prototypes evolved from a modernised version of the aborted Ensign design into entirely new designs that owed more to the influence of other automobile designers around the world than to anything that Armstrong Siddeley had ever produced before. Just two distinctive aspects of traditional Armstrong Siddeley design remained, although with major changes. Firstly the traditional sphinx mascot was changed to an elongated art deco-style sphinx head, and secondly the Vee-shaped radiator grille was less pronounced and the slats were now horizontal rather than vertical – perhaps influenced by the American Cord? The men working on the new car project had been extraordinarily busy and productive. The naming of the new models had been decided and hinted at in Armstrong Siddeley advertisements during the latter stages of the war. Various advertisements had featured wartime aircraft which Hawker Siddeley had produced while the accompanying copy stated that the quality of these aircraft would also be carried forwards into the new Armstrong Siddeley cars after the war. The aircraft that were featured were the Hurricane, Lancaster and Typhoon.

The first new 16 hp cars after the war were the Hurricane and the Lancaster. Another model, the Tempest, was not continued beyond the prototypes stage and many Armstrong Siddeley enthusiasts have argued about its appearance for many years. The picture reproduced here is believed to be the definitive answer to this quest. It was found by the

Unsurprisingly this particular Armstrong Siddeley model never went on sale. It is believed to be a company hack that was hastily assembled for wartime use. You may not be dismayed to learn that it has not survived. (ASHT)

This undated photograph probably shows an early prototype for the post-war range of cars. Stylistically it seems to be a halfway house between the last of the pre-war cars with separate headlamps and vertical radiator slats, but the overall shape is similar to the post-war Lancaster. The registration number FYV 9 was one of three used during the war for the development of post-war cars. (ASHT)

This stylish prototype dashboard dates from 1943. Note the neat inclusion of a radio at the lower edge. It was never used in a production car. (AHT)

A roadside hoarding from 1944 which gave a good indication of the shape of cars to come. (ASHT)

A prototype for the Lancaster built during the Second World War. Note the shape and position of the mascot. (ASHT)

This is the real Tempest according to the factory envelope in which the negative is stored. It is dated 1947 and has a longer wheelbase than the 16 hp cars that were available at that time. When an 18 hp limousine was released it looked more like the Whitley whereas this car looks like a stretched Lancaster. (ASHT)

Armstrong Siddeley Heritage Trust among the collection of company negatives that it acquired a few years ago, in its original sleeve, marked 'Tempest'. This elegant car appears to be larger than the two other new 16 hp cars, certainly with greater headroom in the cabin, and was possibly to be thought of as the limousine version of the 16 hp. If it had been put into production its presumed increased weight over the smaller Hurricane and Lancaster would probably have made its progress regal rather than satisfying. The second prototype pictured, which is marked as Mr Chapman's car on the negative, has been cited as the mythical Tempest by some historians, as have various drawings and small-scale clay mock-ups. There may be an element of truth in all these claims. Perhaps the company did intend to roll out another model called the Tempest, but having considered the cars pictured here then decided that introducing another model would be too ambitious as there were problems in obtaining materials for the cars already in production.

The Hurricanes and Lancasters were put into production as quickly as possible. In May 1945 tooling and plant to make the required production line was started with the fairly ambitious target of producing the new cars by Christmas, or early in the New Year in 1946. The target was met during December 1945 when the first dozen cars were completed. The Hurricane was a four-seater, two-door, drophead coupe of respectable performance. The Lancaster shared its chassis with the Hurricane but the bodywork, again rather elegant, was made by Mulliners. The four-seat, four-door car had a particularly comfortable interior and weighed and cost a few pounds more than the Hurricane. The announcement of these two new cars, the first new models made in Britain after the war, attracted a lot of favourable coverage in the motoring press. This press interest was no surprise as motoring

This early Hurricane with the hood raised shows how rear-seat passengers were left in the dark. (ASHT)

The production version of the Lancaster. The coachwork was by Mulliner of Birmingham (not to be confused with H. J. Mulliner) and the car cost a little more than the Hurricane and the Typhoon.

journalists had been starved of new cars to write about for years. It was immediately clear that both models were ideal for the wealthy owner who enjoyed driving himself, though neither car was really suited to chauffeur driving, but in the long period of austerity after the war not many people could afford to retain the services of a chauffeur. While many people longed for a new car the actual chance of buying one was very much restricted to those with deep pockets and a good deal of patience. The government policy of 'export or die' required manufacturers to export at least 50 per cent of their products in an effort to deal with enormous post-war debts, particularly those owed to America. The British economy was in a mess and the government controlled the distribution of sorely needed raw materials to industry. 'Export or die' was both an exhortation and a threat.

Two of the first Hurricanes made were immediately shipped to America to fulfil an order from International Motors in Los Angeles. The cars, one with manual synchromesh gearbox and the other with a Wilson pre-selector gearbox and Newton centrifugal clutch, were unloaded in New York and then driven 3,500 miles across America in a variety of temperatures from sub-zero to desert heat and over a variety of road surfaces. When conditions allowed they cruised at 50–60 mph. The cars were driven by Roger Barlow, the head of International Motors, and George Kirby, chief test driver for Armstrong Siddeley Motors. The run was entirely successful and Mr Kirby experimented with different carburettor settings in the various climatic conditions – a useful opportunity as the long-distance testing of the new cars had been undertaken in the more restricted range of UK temperatures. Although this journey went well, and attracted more favourable coverage in the British motoring press, sales of these cars were poor in the USA, where drivers preferred much larger, lower revving engines. The comparative economy of the 16 hp engine was of little interest where petrol was so cheap. Incidentally, the manual synchromesh gearbox was the first manual gearbox to be fitted to an Armstrong Siddeley since 1931, although there was no synchromesh on first gear. In practice the lack of first-gear synchromesh was of little consequence and with the comparatively low-gear ratios many drivers only used first gear for hill starts. Although the pre-select gearbox was a little more expensive, it was the choice of most buyers and was seen as one of the advantages of buying an Armstrong Siddeley.

By mid-1946 another body choice was added to the 16 hp cars, this time named after the Typhoon aeroplane. This model was virtually identical to the Hurricane but had a fixed fabric-covered roof and the absence of the hood mechanism allowed for a little more width in the back seat. This model was introduced because Mulliner of Birmingham was unable to keep up with the demand for Lancaster car bodies. Rearward vision was good with a reasonable-size back window plus side windows for the back-seat passengers. One of the disadvantages of the Hurricane is poor rear visibility through a small rear window. Even three quarters rear-view is restricted as the hood, when erected, blanks off the view behind the B post, and this also leaves rear-seat passengers sitting in the dark with hardly any view at all. When the hood is folded down the all-round view is wonderful, although a trifle drafty, which can upset female passengers in particular as expensive hair styles are reduced to the bird nest look. Naturally a gentleman driver would carry sufficient headscarves in the cubby hole to cater for his female passengers' needs. I have described these cars as four seaters but when new they were often described as having space for five people, or even six at a push when fitted with bench front seats unencumbered by a gear stick if the car is fitted with a pre-selector gearbox. In the twenty-first century, people commonly have larger posteriors and to fit a third person in the front or the back is a bit of a squash and uncomfortable for long journeys.

The interior use of highly polished wood and leather throughout the range (and a certain amount of leather cloth in places) made the cabins of all models a very comforting world for the cars' occupants. While travelling the owner could relish informing his passengers about some of the car's features, including built-in jacks which folded down and raised the

A 16 hp Typhoon. This model joined the Hurricane and Lancaster in 1946, and from 1949 it received the 18 hp engine, although most of the 18 hp versions were exported.

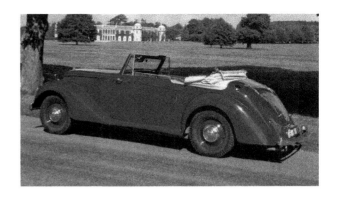

Once the top is folded down on a Hurricane everyone gets a good view. This 1950 18 hp Hurricane is fitted with the harmonic bumpers; in 1951 they were replaced with the Whitley-type bumpers.

car on either side by the use of a winding handle, warning lights on the dashboard that would indicate a blown bulb or dynamo problems, and a top speed in excess of 70 mph. If the driver cared to demonstrate the maximum speed available the engine noise became apparent and on all but the smoothest roads a simultaneous exhibition of the habit of narrow cross-ply tyres to wander around the road would also be given. Fortunately the four-wheel drum brakes, hydraulic front and mechanical rear make a good job of stopping these 1½-ton cars, but the skinny cross-ply tyres limit effectiveness due to the small amount of rubber in contact with the road.

During 1949 the 2-litre engine in the 16 hp cars was replaced with a bored-out version of 2.3 litres that provided 18 hp. This small difference in capacity gave a noticeable improvement in performance while fuel consumption remained virtually unchanged in the low twenties per gallon. Unfortunately the gearbox ratios also remained unchanged, causing the engine to run at higher speeds than desirable when travelling at speed. Some owners of these cars have since increased the ratio of the differential and report a much more pleasant driving experience when travelling at higher speeds, while some other owners have fitted overdrive with equally beneficial results. The 18 hp cars also featured redesigned dashboards with even more polished wood to admire.

A 1950 change to the model range was the addition of the Whitley, a semi-razor-edged four-door, four-seat saloon car which looked more modern than the Lancaster. With its factory-built body its price was kept to £975 plus purchase tax, which matched the price of the Hurricane and the Typhoon and undercut the price of the Lancaster by £25. With purchase tax added the price of the factory-bodied cars was £1,246 11s 8d – roughly double the average annual pay at the time. This model proved popular with customers as its more modern styling helped rejuvenate the 16/18 hp range, which had been on sale for five years and was looking a bit dated in comparison with some other makers' cars that were coming onto the market. To an extent a modern appearance was not a primary concern with customers who looked to Armstrong Siddeley for craftsmanship, reliability and a certain conservative air of respectability. The post-war model range answered these requirements with ease as these cars were over-engineered as a matter of company practice. With good regular maintenance the 16/18 hp engines can have a very long life, with 250,000 miles and more being attained by some of them. Regular oil and filter changes contribute hugely to longevity, as does keeping the coolant system in good order and regularly oiling the air intake mesh for the carburettor to keep dust away from the engine's innards.

An Armstrong Siddeley Whitley. This model was available from 1950 to early 1954 and was always supplied with the 18 hp engine, and could be ordered in four-light or six-light versions. It effectively replaced the Lancaster, which went out of production in 1952.

With the popularity of the Whitley sales for the Typhoon and Lancaster were reduced and the Lancaster was phased out, but the Hurricane still sold well. The complete range of 18 hp cars was stopped in 1953. By then the Whitley was available in its first four-light configuration or as a six-light body that was subsequently introduced. The Hurricane had lost its original back end which included a separate spare wheel compartment behind the harmonic bumper. This design looked neat, if dated, but accessing the spare wheel was a slow procedure. The revised rear end from the Whitley was a less fussy design and provided greater boot space on a shelf with the spare wheel located underneath, making access to it easy.

These then were the basic four 16/18 hp models, but as ever with Armstrong Siddeley variations on the theme were made as well. In 1949 two utility or pick-up models were produced and ran for three years. This unlikely sidetrack is thought to have been inspired by Australian dealers during a period when the antipodean wool trade was booming. Australia and to a lesser extent New Zealand were providing good export markets, and if sheep shearers and other agricultural users wanted an upmarket pick-up, the factory was keen to fill the bill – all export orders were very welcome and around 60 per cent of the utility models were sold to Australia. Other overseas markets included Chile, Venezuela and the USA.

Two models were available: the Station Coupe had a rear bench seat in a spartan cabin with a small load area behind, while the Utility Coupe had a smaller cabin with one bench seat and a larger load area behind. In total a little over 1,700 of these models were made, but only around 100 were sold in the home market. The dashboards were painted metal pressings as were the door cappings, and the floor was covered with rubber mats. The vehicles cost around two thirds of the price of one of the standard car models, but even so they were still more expensive than most of the utility vehicles in the same market segment. With the majority of these load carriers being sold overseas survivors in the UK are rare and now they command a premium because of their rarity.

The 18 hp range was further extended with the announcement in 1950 of a long wheelbase limousine built by Burlington, the in-house coachbuilders, as were all standard bodies on Armstrong Siddeley cars at that time, apart from the Lancaster, which was made by Mulliner. The limousine body was capable of carrying up to eight people and was usually fitted with a glass division behind the driver. The driver's seat was covered in tough leather while the passengers' cabin was finished in West of England cloth or fine leather. The passengers were also given a heater while the driver had to make do with heat soak from the engine, but this

The Station Coupe, which had a small bench seat behind the driver and passenger.

The Utility Coupe, with a slightly larger load area but no rear seats. Both Coupes were built on the 18 hp chassis but the interiors were spartan by Armstrong Siddeley standards. (ASHT)

The interior of the Coupe pick-ups was very basic, with no wood trim, glovebox lid or heater. To get more fresh air (and outback dust) into the cabin small flaps could be opened by the levers seen on the lower sides of the cabin. (ASHT)

An 18 hp chassis with a coach-built shooting brake body by Bonnallack of East London. Bill Smith's book *Armstrong Siddeley Motors* says that there were possibly five of these shooting brakes built but the records are unclear. (ASHT)

One of two landaulettes versions of the limousine built on the long wheelbase 18 hp, one of which was built for the Sultan of Zanzibar.

An 18 hp longwheel base limousine was hardly an obvious choice to enter in the 1952 RAC Rally but this one, waiting to climb Hardknott Pass, completed the rally successfully. (Hawker Siddeley Review)

The 18 hp limousine was not ostentatious, but it was a very practical vehicle and was the first post-war car that fitted the needs of the carriage trade. (ASHT)

probably sufficed as the engine had to propel a car weighing around 2 tons when loaded with passengers. The appearance of the limousine is something of an acquired taste that not everyone acquires, but the limousine was a practical proposition for the carriage trade. It also sold well to councils seeking a suitable mayoral conveyance at less than Rolls-Royce prices and to funeral directors needing capacious cars for a cortege. The biggest single customer was Godrey Davis who used a fleet over fifty of these limousines for their chauffeur-driven service.

Final variations on the 16/18 hp theme were supplied by outside coachbuilders using these chassis. In the 1940s and '50s individual buyers who wanted special coach-built bodies were uncommon but nonetheless 112 cars were sold in chassis form and what happened next is not known for many of these cars. Dutch coachbuilder Pennock did their own version of the Hurricane which was very similar to the factory version but just a little better looking with the appearance and practicality improved by the fitting of windows for the back-seat passengers. A batch of twenty-eight chassis were sent to Denmark to be bodied as taxis, but little is known about these cars. Bonnallack & Sons in East London are reputed to have made six shooting brake bodies on 16/18 chassis, although the number has not been substantiated. In 1952 Ghia exhibited a good-looking and more modern take on the 18 hp chassis.

Dutch coachbuilders Pennock made their own version of the Hurricane. It was 2 inches longer than the factory version but the main difference was the provision of windows for the back-seat passengers. Pennock bodies were fitted to twenty-six 16/18 hp chassis before the company ceased trading in 1953.

This 18 hp chassis was given elegant coachwork by Ghia in 1952, but by then Armstrong Siddeley was devoting its attention to a replacement for the 18 hp cars. (ASHT)

6

The Beginning of the Sapphire Years

When the 16/18 hp range of cars was phased out in 1953 it had served the company well for eight years but was looking distinctly dated, and its engine, with its roots in a pre-war design, had lasted well as the face of motoring changed. The replacement car was so completely different that for a while it sold alongside the last of the 18 hp cars as the old and the new appealed to different market segments.

The car division had been working towards an entirely new car to replace the 16/18 hp cars for some time.

One possibility that was considered was to buy the ailing Lagonda car company and to badge a new saloon car that they were developing as an Armstrong Siddeley. This idea was pre-empted when David Brown bought Lagonda before Armstrong Siddeley had even put in a bid. Next, W. O. Bentley was engaged on a three-year contract to design a new car and engine, but sadly this plan failed too. Poor communications and muddled thinking on the part of Armstrong Siddeley resulted in W. O. Bentley producing a prototype car with a Lagonda-derived engine that Armstrong Siddeley did not really want. The contract was terminated with little to show for it by either party.

Apart from the expense incurred by the aborted project, the delay meant that Armstrong Siddeley now needed to design and develop a new car and engine as quickly as possible. In short order the following elements were put together:

- Parts of the 16/18 hp chassis had been incorporated into Bentley's design, but his chassis was bigger, stronger and lighter than the old 16/18 hp chassis. Torsion bar suspension was replaced with coil-spring suspension on the front and the usual leaf spring on the rear.

- The new power unit designed and built, in an oft-quoted three months, by Fred Allard was a straight six-cylinder 3.4-litre engine. Again, it may have retained vestigial elements of Bentley's work but they were more in the theory than in the hardware. This engine was a single overhead camshaft design rather than Bentley's double overhead camshaft design, and it was designed to convey a large and luxurious body.

The all-new body was a very big move away from the 16/18 hp series of cars. It was large, luxurious car, and aimed squarely at the professional classes who wished to impress, although it also had a very good turn of speed for long-distance touring. It could also seat six people in

After post-war austerity the Sapphire 346 emerged to take Armstrong Siddeley firmly back into the luxury car market. It sold well – nearly 7,700 cars in a little over six years – and was sometimes called the poor man's Rolls-Royce.

In 1952 Vincents of Reading made six prototype Sapphire 346 limousines referred to as 'experimental for testing'. In appearance it seems to be a cross between the Tempest (see previous chapter) and the production Sapphire 346 Limousine that became available in 1955. (ASHT)

relative comfort if a bench seat was fitted in the front rather than two individual front seats, and the boot was much larger than that of the previous 16/18 hp cars. The first production models were ready just in time for the 1952 Motor Show, where it was launched as the Sapphire 346, with the figures denoting engine capacity and the number of cylinders. The Sapphire name was still aviation based, but whereas the previous model names looked back to aircraft of the Second World War, the Sapphire derived its name from the jet engines made by Armstrong Siddeley that powered a whole raft of military aircraft. To further celebrate this link to the aeronautical side of its maker the sphinx mascot was also changed. The long, slim art deco head that had graced the 16/18 hp cars was replaced by a much shorter sphinx head and behind it two wing stumps protruded, each supporting a jet engine. Finally, a stylised fin was mounted on top of the engines. Surely such a mix of ancient myth and modern technology has never been, before or since, combined in a motor car mascot. It was totally mad, and yet much beloved by Armstrong Siddeley owners.

By the start of 1953 the Sapphire 346 was selling alongside the last batches of the 18 hp cars, and in good numbers by Armstrong Siddeley standards. As it was so different to the earlier cars they continued to sell right up until the start of 1954 when the final 18 hp cars left the showrooms. Sales of around sixty to seventy Sapphire 346s a week showed that Armstrong Siddeley had successfully identified a niche market that wanted an impressive and prestigious car but either could not afford the likes of a Rolls-Royce or shied away from the ostentatious image of such cars. They probably made a wise choice because the Sapphire was considered by many people to be at least the equal of the Bentley Mark Six or the equivalent Rolls-Royce offering. Indeed, some people thought that the Armstrong Siddeley was both quieter and smoother than its more expensive competitors in the luxury-class market. Like them the Sapphire was undeniably an upright statement of British craftsmanship that appealed to the professional classes. However, it was very different, and perhaps a little old-fashioned looking when compared with the likes of Jaguar, and over the next few years the much more modern-looking and high-performing models from other makers reached a widening market while the market for the Sapphire 346 gradually diminished.

The Sapphire 346 was quite grand enough to be driven by a chauffeur and the car responded well to driving gently around town before picking up its skirts and proceeding at high speed on the open road. However it was not designed for rapid progress around corners as its high centre of gravity and soft suspension could provoke excessive body roll and squealing tyres if they were taken too fast. Driven as intended the Sapphire 346 gives its driver a tremendous feeling of well-being and rear-seat passengers are cossetted in armchair-like comfort with a great deal of legroom.

Naturally with Armstrong Siddeley a continuous stream of improvements were made to the Sapphire 346 during its production run from late 1952 right up to the last cars made in 1958. Some changes were minor while other changes were more significant. To list all the modifications would take up a lot of space, but it is worth mentioning the introduction of the Mark Two model in 1954 which, apart from slight visual changes in chrome trim and interior trim design, introduced a revised braking set-up with larger brake drums and Layton Dewandre servo assistance, and flashing indicator lamps rather than semaphore arms. The Mark Two also introduced the option of an automatic gearbox for the first time in an Armstrong Siddeley, alongside the pre-selector and manual gearbox options. The automatic gearbox had four forward speeds, and by the standards of the time it gave very smooth gear changes, although it does not compare well with the sublime smoothness of modern automatics. Many buyers chose the automatic box for its ease of use and plenty of the Sapphire 346s that come onto the market today still have them. If they have been well maintained they are still a joy to use, but those that have not been well looked after are often referred to as jerkomatics. One aspect of maintenance that is often overlooked by owners who fail to read their handbooks is that topping up the gearbox needs to be carried out while the engine is running. Failure to adhere to this results in running without sufficient gearbox lubrication and causes rapid wear, noise and jerky gear changes. However these are strong gearboxes and can run for years if the wear is not too advanced, and smooth gear changes can usually be achieved by the driver anticipating each gear change and momentarily lifting off the accelerator while the change is made, avoiding a jerk as the next gear is engaged. With any of the gearbox options a well-cared for car will glide quietly and smoothly if everything is in good order.

The Sapphire 346 looks impressive from any angle with its sweeping lines. It was popular in its day and remains popular with owners today who appreciate its comfort and ability to keep up with modern traffic.

Other optional choices for the Sapphire 346 were a twin carburettor version which increased top speed to an attainable 100 mph – a questionable benefit bearing in mind the limitations of cross-ply tyres, and most people found the 90 mph top speed of the single carburettor version quite sufficient. A more useful option came along in 1955 when Girling power steering was offered. The Sapphire 346 has very heavy steering at slow speeds, which can make parking in a tight space something of a physical workout. The amount of power assistance used is adjustable by a simple sliding control on the dashboard, thus help can be easily provided when needed and then reduced once the car has gathered a little speed. This option is even more of a boon today when many drivers choose to run on radial tyres. Retrofitting the Girling system is quite possible but the parts needed are exceedingly rare. Four-and six-light versions of the body were also available according to taste.

When Thomas Sopwith senior was around seventy years old, but still an active man, he expressed a desire to see the new M1 motorway. One of the Hawker Siddeley fleet of Sapphire 346s complete with a chauffeur gave him a ride along the newly opened road at a sedate speed, but when the chauffeur pulled off the motorway to turn round for the journey back Sopwith insisted on taking the wheel and the chauffeur was relegated to the back seat, next to one of the other group directors. Sopwith promptly accelerated to over 100 mph for the return run along the motorway, much to the alarm of his passengers.

The other major option available from 1955 was a long chassis limousine. Although the chassis was only extended by 19 inches, the limousine version of the Sapphire 346 has a commanding and regal appearance. It shared no body panels with the standard-length car as the waist was raised and the cabin height was also increased. The driver's compartment was much the same as the standard saloon version, although the windscreen was larger to fit the enlarged body. The passenger cabin behind the glass division was very luxurious, trimmed in West of England cloth or leather at the owner's choice. It also had a central roof light and side lights controlled by the passengers, who also had control of their own heater outlets. Occasional seats fold neatly into the front partition. This car was popular with the carriage trade and for any use when formal cars were needed, and they were also popular with the chauffeurs who drove them because their comfort was looked after almost as well as that of the passengers making these large cars are a pleasure to drive.

The Sapphire 346 Limousine is a large, imposing vehicle.

A 346 Limousine with an enlarged radiator grille for a large air-conditioning unit, and a windscreen sun shield. This car was built to order for an unknown customer, possibly the Shah of Persia. (ASHT)

Given that Armstrong Siddeley had reclaimed a place providing cars for the upper echelons of society with the introduction of the Sapphire 346, it was very surprising when they produced another variant on the standard 346 chassis in 1955 – a rough and tough-looking pick-up truck that would have been ideal for Lara Croft had she been around at that time. This distinctive pick-up looked like the offspring of a union between the Sapphire 346 and a military desert truck. The intended market was the oil industry in the Middle East and one or more customers there liked the vehicle enough to buy forty-four of them. There were no takers in Australia where many of the earlier pick-ups had been sold, but that is hardly surprising as the native Holden pick-ups had pretty well sewn up the market for two-wheel-drive pick-ups and Land Rover had entered the fray with four-wheel-drive capability. This stylish-looking pick-up was stripped of all luxury with painted metal replacing chrome and polished wood. The radiator grille was a utilitarian affair and the customary sphinx had declined the invitation to ride upon it. There is one survivor of this model, current condition unknown.

One of the forty-four Sapphire 346 pick-ups built for the Middle Eastern oil industry. They featured strengthened and raised suspension and chrome was replaced with painted parts. There was a forty-fifth pick-up made, which was last seen in the UK in the 1970s. There are no known survivors from the Middle East batch. (ASHT)

The front view of the rugged pick-up with its mesh radiator grille. The sphinx decided not to travel to the Middle East. (ASHT)

Disregarding the pick-up, it can be easily appreciated that the Sapphire 346 was a smart car for the professional classes and a world away from the sporting motorist's inclinations. So there was another surprise when garage owner and motorsport journalist Mike Couper asked Armstrong Siddeley if they would lend him a Sapphire 346 for him to drive in the 1954 Monte Carlo Rally. Mike Couper had made it an annual habit to make such a request for the loan of a car for this event from various carmakers and they often complied in the hopes of getting good publicity. The request went to Board level and was agreed with. Couper never expected to win on performance but he had his eyes on awards for safety, comfort, quality of coachwork and level of preparedness for the rally. Entry for these events at someone else's expense must have made an exciting change from watching over his St Albans car showroom in the quiet month of January. The rally went well and although the car was damaged along the way, Couper managed to get the damage partially repaired before judging for the various concours classes began. The Sapphire 346 was awarded the *Grand Prix de Securite*. Armstrong Siddeley naturally made much of this award in publicity.

Later in 1954 the company decided that it would compete for team and concours prizes in the 1955 running of the rally. To this end three cars would be entered as a team and the Couper car should concentrate solely on concours awards. Although the cars were in

Mike Couper's Sapphire 346 prepared for the 1955 Monte Carlo Rally. Note headlamp wash/wipers and windscreen interior with screen heater, lower internal Perspex strip to aid screen demisting, an adjustable spotlight and exterior with thermometer. (ASHT)

standard form they were all subject to a great deal of preparation before the event. The engines were removed and stripped down before being rebuilt to ensure maximum reliability and efficiency. Lengthy bench testing ensured that the engines were well run-in before the event. In addition the Couper car had a whole host of assorted accessories fitted to catch the eye of the *confort* and *securité* (comfort and safety) judging panel at the end of the event. Most of these accessories were entirely sensible while some were verging on the bizarre – a container by the engine connected to the cooling system to heat tins of soup and a tap for personal washing complete with sponge and towel, and boxes in front of each rear wheel containing sand, which could be set to empty this sand for enhanced wheel grip. You will not be surprised to learn that these ideas never made it onto production cars. After a good deal of time and expense preparing for the rally the results were no better than for the previous year with Couper's car winning the *Concours de Confort*, while the team entry had gone by the boards early on when one of the team cars was severely damaged skidding off the road in England before it even reached France. The Armstrong Siddeley board of directors were not pleased with the outcome as they felt that what little good publicity had been gained from the event did not justify the expense of the exercise. The competitors' expenses were repaid after close scrutiny. This was the last official factory entry into any sort of motor sport event.

The Sapphire 346 sold well in Britain and as usual in reasonable numbers in Australia and New Zealand. Elsewhere export figures were disappointing. A lengthy demonstration trip with two Sapphire 346s around America achieved very little. A complete knock-down kit of a four-light Sapphire 346 was sent to Minerva in Belgium, which they modified into a convertible with a power-operated hood, and it is believed that they also fitted a strengthening cross piece between the B posts to counter body flexing introduced by the absence of a rigid roof. Apparently this was insufficient to solve the problem and the only known example was subsequently converted back into a saloon car. There have long been rumours that three or even four of these convertibles were made but none are thought to have survived, apart from the one that was made back into a saloon car.

Almost all of the Sapphire 346s were sold as standard saloons. A few went to coachbuilders for conversion to estate cars or shooting brakes but there are none left in

A Sapphire 346 estate car with coachwork made by Appleyards of Leeds. It is thought that they made two of these cars but it is not known if either of them survive. (ASHT)

An ambulance built on a Sapphire 346 long wheelbase chassis – ideal transport for the discerning casualty. A number of hearses were also made on the same chassis and at least one is still in use. (ASHT)

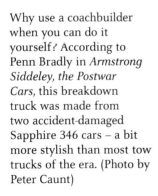

Why use a coachbuilder when you can do it yourself? According to Penn Bradly in *Armstrong Siddeley, the Postwar Cars*, this breakdown truck was made from two accident-damaged Sapphire 346 cars – a bit more stylish than most tow trucks of the era. (Photo by Peter Caunt)

Tom Sopwith Junior's *Sphinx* racing car complete with its sphinx head mascot. Before he sold the *Sphinx* the engine and gearbox were removed and put into the Sapphire 346 behind for saloon car racing. Both cars were road registered even in racing trim. (ASHT).

running condition at the moment, and the last reports concerning derelict conversions suggest that they have probably not been saved.

However, long wheelbase chassis did go to various coachbuilders to make mainly ambulances and hearses. A pick-up body was also produced on the long chassis for a machine tool maker. With a large Perspex dome over the load area, it was used as a mobile exhibition platform. This vehicle, without its Perspex cover, still exists in the ownership of the Armstrong Siddeley Owners Club. Over the last couple of decades it has been put on the road for display purposes either by the club or in the care of the Rolls-Royce Heritage Trust. Although currently somewhat patinated, its very large load area is an unusual sight.

One 346 engine had a particularly interesting life. In the early 1950s, Tom Sopwith Junior, the son of the chairman of Hawker Siddeley, was head of the experimental department of the car division of Armstrong Siddeley Motors, and he wanted to go motor racing. To this end he commissioned a lightweight sports racing car from Allard that was fitted with a two-seater body looking quite a lot like the Aston Martin DB3S. Power came from a heavily modified 346 engine coupled to a Wilson pre-select gearbox. The engine modifications included a specially made high-lift camshaft, triple Weber double throat carburettors and a specially made exhaust manifold to improve gas flow. The development and testing of this car was undertaken by a team of factory volunteers working with young Tom, all in their own time rather than company time, allegedly. The car was named the *Sphinx* and Tom drove it enthusiastically for a couple of seasons. In the first season results were good with a number of wins and class wins, but also some disappointments caused by overheating. The car was competitive in its first year when pitted against Aston Martin DB3s and Jaguar C Types but soon became outclassed by the introduction of cars like the D Type Jaguar. The big manufacturers were happy to spend money on continuous development of new racing cars, but Tom did not have the resources to develop his *Sphinx*. He did continue driving for a while in saloon car races and for these he took the engine and gearbox from the *Sphinx* and fitted them into a Sapphire 346. The *Sphinx* was sold and its new owner raced it with a Jaguar engine and gearbox. Tom's racing Sapphire 346 became rather worn after hard campaigning and was scrapped. Tom continued saloon car racing in other cars and was narrowly beaten to victory in the first British Touring Cars Championship. Recently the *Sphinx* has been purchased by a new owner, who is working on fitting a Sapphire 346 engine and pre-selector gearbox to original racing specifications. It would be wonderful to see this car racing again.

Two Smaller Sapphires and the Most Polished Sapphire

During his time at Armstrong Siddeley, Tom Sopwith Junior did a lot of work on developing two other Sapphire models: the 234 and the 236. These externally identical models are often referred to as baby Sapphires, which is reasonable given that they are much smaller than the Sapphire 346. They are also often thought of as warmed-over 18 hp cars with an ugly new body – an impression strengthened by the use of the art deco sphinx's head mascot that had been used on the 16/18 hp cars. These thoughts denigrate cars that have a lot to recommend themselves, as well as some less fortunate facets. It is worth considering both the good and the bad in these cars rather than just writing them off as some sort of mistake.

The Sapphire 236 was launched in the 1955 Motor Show, as was the Jaguar 2.4 litre. The Jaguar attracted a great deal of attention which eclipsed the less sensational-looking new car from Armstrong Siddeley. The appearance of the baby Sapphires is not their strong suit, although by Armstrong Siddeley standards it was a leap into the future and had had extensive wind tunnel testing, which in turn helped improve performance and fuel consumption, as well as reducing wind noise on the move. There is a hoary old chestnut that the roofline on the baby Sapphires was raised by a couple of inches to accommodate occupants wearing bowler hats. Whether true or not the height of the cabin does seem a little out of proportion, and may

The baby Sapphire 236 (the 234 looks the same). Both models are now rare as sales when new were poor, and good examples are sought after.

The baby Sapphires all carried the same sleek sphinx head mascot that was used on the Hurricane, Lancaster, Typhoon and Whitley.

have been improved by being a little lower, but if the baby Sapphires are compared with Rover P4s then they have nothing to be embarrassed about. Calling the baby Sapphires warmed-over 16/18 hp cars is completely inaccurate. The cruciform base was similar to the 346 chassis design, although on a smaller scale, but it was much lighter than the earlier chassis while still being impressively strong. Servo-assisted brakes and improved suspension were also new; in fact, just about the only parts that looked similar to the earlier cars were the 2.3-litre straight six (236) engine and the smart wooden dashboard. The engine was indeed a development of the old 18 hp engine but internally much improved with higher compression ratio, better valve design and so forth. In its new incarnation the engine was quieter, smoother and developed an extra 10 bhp to give an output of 85 bhp. Incidentally the 236 engine can be retrofitted into the earlier 16/18 hp cars with relative ease, a modification that many people have adopted with good results. The downside is that spare 236 engines in any condition are thin on the ground but they are generally well worth rebuilding if condition permits.

The bodywork was lighter than on the previous models due to the use of thinner steel and many panels being made of Hiduminium alloy. The end result was a comfortable family car that handled well and topped out at around 85 mph – a very respectable performance for the period. And that was just the low-power model. The Sapphire 234 was identical to the 236 outside apart from discrete badging for the cognoscenti, but under the bonnet there was a different 2.3-litre engine, this time of four cylinders (hence 234). This was the high-performance baby Sapphire, for although the engine had the same displacement it was a development of the engine from the 346 engine – basically the same engine as the larger Sapphire but with two cylinders amputated. This may sound like a small and pointless exercise, but much work had been carried out on the internal design of this engine too and had resulted in a power output of 120 bhp, which was only 5 bhp down on the 3.4-litre engine. The end result was true sports car-like performance with a top speed of 100 mph – indeed, it was something of a wolf in sheep's clothing. Tom Sopwith Junior said that it took a lot of development work to get this performance out of the new four-cylinder engine, and it is thought that the results shook Jaguar to the extent that it may have been part of the impetus behind their production of the Mark 2 Jaguar with its engine options up to 3.8 litres.

As it happened they need not have worried too much because the public did not take to the two baby Sapphires and sales figures were poor. Over three years just over 1,400 of the baby

The Sapphire 236 had the 2.3-litre straight six engine with a single Stromberg carburettor...

... while the Sapphire 234 had the 2.3-litre four-cylinder engine with twin SU carburettors.

Sapphires were sold, with the four-cylinder 234 selling around 800 cars while the remaining 600 cars had the 236 engine. Sales figures could have possibly been increased if the factory had responded to dealership orders promptly, but they did not and the dealers could not sell cars that they did not have. The factory never set up a dedicated production line for the small Sapphires, instead fitting them in between batches on the Sapphire 346 line when they could. Production of both the 234 and the 236 ended in 1958.

Various transmission options were available on the 234 and 236 with synchromesh being the preferred option for most, especially with overdrive when it became available. Another option that gained favour for a while was the Lockheed Manumatic gearbox, which was a sort of halfway house to an automatic gearbox. The driver selects the required gear and as he does so the weight of the driver's hand on the gear stick operates a micro-switch built into the gearbox. The switch actuates two vacuum servos which disengage the clutch and the accelerator and the gear is changed. When the driver's hand is removed from the gear stick the micro-switch re-engages the clutch and the accelerator – a system much easier to use than to describe. The baby Sapphires have similar interiors and are light and comfortable. The dashboards are traditional polished wood, but the 234 has the addition of a large rev counter neatly added.

One big weakness of both the small Sapphires was destruction by corrosion, as rain drainage was poorly designed, but worse was the electrolytic corrosion action caused by the interaction of aluminium alloy and steel where they were joined together. Simple precautions to treat these different materials where they were in contact would have saved many cars now long since

A car whose whereabouts is unknown is this Sapphire 234, clothed by Michelotti. It is assumed to be long since scrapped. (ASHT)

A 1953 concept picture for a new Armstrong Siddeley model, possibly an alternative for the Sapphire 234/236 cars. (ASHT)

scrapped. Comparatively few have survived and perhaps because of this low survival rate good examples are sought after when they come onto the market. The sporting Sapphire 234 tended to attract more enthusiastic drivers who were keen to use the power available, and probably for this reason even fewer of this version survive, thus attracting higher prices when they do come up for sale. That said they fetch significantly less than Jaguars of the same period and in similar condition, and they surely make an interesting alternative to Mr Lyon's cars.

During the 1950s many plans for new cars were made and then abandoned. In 1958 all of the different Sapphires made up until then went out of production, and another Sapphire went on to the showrooms: the Star Sapphire. This was to be a stopgap model until something rather more modern for the 1960s could be put into production.

For a stopgap model the Star Sapphire was a remarkably polished car in all aspects. It looked an awful lot like the Sapphire 346, although no panels are a common fit. The waistline and roofline of the Star Sapphire are lower and give the car a sleek and refined appearance. The radiator grille is a little lower too so that the bonnet lip covers the top of it, and all the doors are front hinged.

The Star Sapphire had been developed by taking a 346 and modifying it panel by panel and part by part. The car used for this development work was TDU 707, which is currently in the hands of the designer's son and, although it now requires some restoration before it can be put back on the road, it was still actively used until a few years ago. In its current state it is partly

The Star Sapphire, the last and the best Armstrong Siddeley model. It is like a Sapphire 346 but sleeker, more comfortable and with superior performance. This is a highly sought-after car.

a 346 but mostly a Star. During development work it was estimated that it covered a quarter of a million miles; it was then rebuilt and refurbished as necessary and was exhibited at the Motor Show as one of the two new Stars on display. After much use by its designer, Alex Rice, he finally bought it from the company for personal use. It is now estimated to have completed more than 400,000 miles, although it may be difficult to find many parts that have been there since the first mile was recorded.

The inside of the Star Sapphire has the sort of opulence that Armstrong Siddeley used to build into cars specially made at great expense for royalty and wealthy VIPs, but in the Star Sapphire it comes as standard. The traditional high standards of craftsmanship in wood and leather are elevated to make a supremely comfortable car. The cabin is slightly narrower than that on the Sapphire 346 – all that luxurious upholstery does take up some space, after all – but it can seat five people in comfort, or four people in luxury.

Passenger comfort and safety is enhanced by improved suspension and the inclusion of front disc brakes, though rear brakes are still drum type. Performance is improved by an enlarged 4.0-litre version of the 3.4-litre engine, and the bigger engine includes some of the design improvements made to the Sapphire 234 engine. A correctly maintained car will cruise all day at speeds well in excess of the legal limit and will easily keep up with twenty-first-century traffic on all types of roads. Power-assisted steering and a very smooth automatic gearbox, the only

The dashboard in a Star Sapphire. Note that the veneer on the glovebox lid and the instrument panel are matched to the surrounding veneer. The heater controls were normally fitted where the radio sits, but to cater for the move Armstrong Siddeley produced the wooden heater control surround seen here.

transmission available on this model, make the driving as effortless for the driver as it is for the car. This stopgap Star Sapphire, a development of the Sapphire 346, is such a leap ahead it has to be considered as a completely new car, and a very successful one at that. It was in production for just two years and only 902 of them were built. A long wheelbase limousine version was made available in 1959 to replace the long wheelbase Sapphire 346 limousines which had continued in production until the Star Sapphire version became available. In early 1960 a Mark Two version of the standard and long wheelbase was about to be released. A prototype of the first Mark Two Star Sapphire saloon had been built and was chiefly identifiable by its twin front headlights arrangements. A long wheelbase limousine Mark Two was also under construction.

There had been plans – many plans – of diverse arrangements and styles to introduce a completely new luxury car in 1958, but when it became obvious that this date could not be met the Star Sapphire was introduced. Plans for a new model were pushed back to 1960 but even this date was not to be met, and when this became clear the improved Star Sapphire Mark Two was being put into production.

These long delays in the introduction of a completely new model were caused by events beyond the control of the Armstrong Siddeley car division.

The final Armstrong Siddeley car was this prototype Star Sapphire. It is still running and in excellent condition. (Photo by Colin Hood, a previous owner of the car)

8

The Axe Falls

For the entire decade of the 1950s, Armstrong Siddeley's car division had been making very small profits or, predominantly, losses, these losses being made up by the very good profits from the aero engine business. By 1960 the aircraft industry was in a mess, partly because there were too many British aircraft companies chasing too little work, and partly because Duncan Sandys' vision of the country's future aviation defence needs resulted in contracts being torn up without notice.

The aviation side of Armstrong Siddeley could no longer afford to keep its little sister with her expensive tastes. In 1960 the accountants put an immediate stop to the production of Armstrong Siddeley cars. One day the cars were in production and the next day they were not. Unfinished cars were scrapped.

Perhaps if reorganisation of car production had been put in hand years before so that it had made at least some profit things would have been different, but there was probably little that could have been done to cut costs in the production of the relatively low volume of hand-built cars. In retrospect the likely cause of the losses made by the cars was that Armstrong Siddeley were trying to compete with Jaguar, Rover and the bigger Humber cars on price while simultaneously aiming to compete with Rolls-Royce and Bentley for build quality.

At the same time that car production was stopped, all future plans for new models were axed as well. A variety of drawings survive of different projected new models and suggested coachwork designs, making it difficult to be sure what would have actually been the car to replace the Star Sapphire had production continued. Armstrong Siddeley historian Bill Smith thinks that the most likely new model would have used a similar chassis to the Star Sapphire and probably the same 4-litre engine but a completely different body style, perhaps similar to the Bentley T Series of cars.

Modern drivers may wonder why Armstrong Siddeley steadfastly kept to the old-fashioned practice of hand building cars when their competitors were embracing the economic benefits of automated production where possible. The answer is easily understood if you are fortunate enough to come across an unmolested Armstrong Siddeley that has been maintained to original standards or a car that has been restored to its original high standards when new. Mechanically the car makes very little noise and has no rattles or other unwanted noises from any part of the drivetrain and suspension. Panel gaps are not good, they are perfect, and the sound of a closing door is a silky-smooth muted click. If you remove a piece of wooden trim, naturally hand finished, you will find the initials of the craftsman who made it written

This concept sketch is unsigned and undated. It is one of a raft of designs that were taken no further. (ASHT)

Armstrong Siddeley
Riverside II

This Riverside 2 design from 1958 by Michelotti looks impressive. Had car production continued beyond 1960, something like this could have been successful and would have modernised the company image. (ASIIT)

in pencil on the underside. Adjoining pieces of veneered wood are pattern matched; it was never a case of just taking the next piece of trim out of a parts bin to fit. In the last sixty years automotive technology has advanced to the stage where smooth, reliable travel at low cost per mile is taken as standard, but only the most expensive cars ever reach the superior old standards for trim and upholstery, and the elegant styling of the best Armstrong Siddeleys will never be repeated.

Telemetry equipment being fitted to a prototype Star Sapphire prior to testing on the company test track at Ansty, just outside Coventry. (Photo: Hawker Siddeley Review)

Although build standards were high it would be wrong to think that Armstrong Siddeley eschewed modern technology. The cars were produced alongside the most modern aircraft engines and draftsmen in the drawing office worked on both automotive and aeronautical products side by side. Also, the company had the benefit of its own test track, developed from the old airfield perimeter road at Ansty, just outside Coventry. The same telemetry technology that was used in aiding aircraft development was also used on later Armstrong Siddeley cars. It was not the sole tool used for development; the hands, ears and eyes of experienced engineers and test drivers played their part too. Once the test track was set up after the Second World War, every new car from the factory was tested there before going to a dealer or a customer. The test drivers would correct slow running on the carburettor but any other faults noticed were recorded on a card for the appropriate department to put right. When this was done the car was put through its paces on the test track again to ensure that the car was ready for its new owner. The only thing to do before the car left the factory was to subject it to a high-pressure water hose to check for any water leaks, and install underlay and carpets, which had been left out until then so that the test drivers could hear the tiniest of unwanted noises.

Although it came as a shock to the workforce when production of Armstrong Siddeley cars was terminated so abruptly, it did not leave a gaping space with tumbleweed blowing across it on the factory floor. At the end of the Star Sapphire weekly production was less than ten cars per week, and next to the space that they had occupied the RAS cars were still in production, and making money for the company.

Even at the height of Star Sapphire production, only a small amount of factory space was needed.

All of the Sunbeam Alpine Mark Ones and a substantial proportion of the Mark Twos were built at Parkside, which was a great help in difficult times when the aviation side of its business was in turmoil. (Photo courtesy of John Willshire)

RAS stood for the Rootes Armstrong Siddeley project and referred to the Sunbeam Alpine sports cars that were being made under contract for Rootes. This project had started in 1957, when Rootes had insufficient space in their own factories to develop and manufacture this new two-seater soft-top sports car. They had reached the stage where they knew what it should look like in outline and that its floor pan would be taken from the Hillman Husky, while its engine would be a version of the 1.5-litre used in a number of Rootes cars. Development into prototypes and then production cars was mostly undertaken by Rootes staff but a lot of detail work and establishing production methods was carried out by Armstrong Siddeley. In another piece of Armstrong Siddeley and Rootes co-operation the companies had worked together to produce a version of the Sapphire 346 engine for the Humber Hawk. Parts of the two engine versions are not interchangeable, but there are obvious similarities externally and internally.

When the new Sunbeam Alpine went into production at the Parkside factory, the car parts arrived from both Rootes and outside contractors. In Parkside the body parts were welded together on jigs and then painted before being completely fitted out and driven under their own power onto car transporters. In fairness this work was best described as a sort of hybrid between full manufacture and just assembling. Therefore the Sunbeam Alpine Mark Ones and early Mark Twos can be considered to contain a certain amount of Armstrong Siddeley DNA within them.

The drawing office also kept busy after the end of Armstrong Siddeley car production. The aviation side of the business, although government policy wanted to decimate the Royal Air Force, was still kept busy on the civilian side. There were also some development projects that never saw the light of day. Two intriguing factory drawings show how a Porsche 1600S engine could be adapted to power a four-wheel-drive amphibious vehicle. The engine was to be mounted transversely amidships and the brakes were to consist of two disc brakes, one on each propshaft. Two small propellers for propulsion in water were also provided. The wheelbase was 80 inches, but no indication of the type of work it was intended for is given.

Another project that never came to fruition was to supply Armstrong Siddeley car engines to Bristol cars. There is one known Armstrong Siddeley Star Sapphire engine fitted in a Bristol 406, but this never came to anything. Shortly afterwards Bristol Cars were sold by Bristol Siddeley Engines and went into private ownership. Thereafter, large Chrysler V8s were fitted as standard from the 407 onwards. The 406 fitted with the 4-litre Armstrong Siddeley engine has been purchased by an Armstrong Siddeley Owners Club member for restoration to its former glory.

When production of Armstrong Siddeley cars stopped, Bristol Siddeley Engines promised that spare parts and servicing for the cars would continue to be available for ten years. Most of the stock of spare parts was transferred to a location in Quinton Road in Coventry, although some parts that were considered excessive for future needs were scrapped. As demand for Armstrong Siddeley parts reduced over time the Quinton Road operation also took on the supply of parts for Alfa Romeo and Mercedes cars. Later Rolls-Royce purchased Bristol Siddeley Engines but the parts and servicing for Armstrong Siddeley cars continued until 1972, at which point Rolls-Royce had decided to bring this operation to a close. There were apparently no potential commercial buyers for this section of Rolls-Royce as a going concern and it seemed likely that the entire remaining stock of Armstrong Siddeley car parts would be lost forever...

9

The Marque Lives On

The Armstrong Siddeley Owners Club was formed in 1960 and took a few years to gain the impetus to keep going. Early members included some senior ex-Armstrong Siddeley Motors staff, notably Walter Henley, who had been in charge of operations at Quinton Road, and Selwyn Sharp, who had been Head of Publicity, as well as the respected motoring writers Bill Boddy and Michael Sedgwick, and a group of dedicated Armstrong Siddeley enthusiasts.

By 1970 the ASOC had overcome some teething troubles, enlarged its membership to over 300 people and established a mostly regular club magazine, *Sphinx*, which was, and still is, a wonderful way to unite members and sustain their interest in the club.

As mentioned at the end of the previous chapter, in 1972 Rolls-Royce had decided to cease its spares and service operation for Armstrong Siddeley cars, which was a cause of consternation for the ASOC. Then something rather remarkable happened – a most fortuitous meeting between Rolls-Royce and the club. Rolls-Royce gave it the opportunity to buy the entire remaining stock of car parts, plus all patents, specifications, drawings and catalogues relating to Armstrong Siddeley cars, and the right to use the name of Armstrong Siddeley Motors. This entire package was offered at a negotiated price of £11,000. This figure equated to approximately £50 per ton of over 200 tons of spare parts, and the replacement value of these parts was estimated at £250,000. Rolls-Royce turned down a higher bid for the package from the Australian Armstrong Siddeley Car Club as they felt that it was more appropriate for the parts to remain in Britain, where the majority of surviving Armstrong Siddeley cars were located. An Extraordinary General Meeting of the ASOC was called and the club agreed to accept the offer and then had to find the money needed as well as premises to house the parts and transportation to remove 220 tons of parts to the premises – and all as quickly as possible because Rolls-Royce urgently needed the space in the Quinton Road premises to expand the training school that was based there.

At this point every Armstrong Siddeley enthusiast should silently thank the work of those early club members who managed to fulfil those daunting requirements. ASOC members made donations to the cause, as did members of Armstrong Siddeley clubs in Holland and New Zealand; other members gave long-term interest-free loans and a shortfall was made up by a bank loan to the club. Suitable premises were located and in just seven weeks thirty lorry-loads of spares had been moved to their new location. As the need to move the parts was urgent, many volunteers would spend their days doing their normal work and then go to Quinton

A view of a small part of the Armstrong Siddeley spare parts held at Quinton Road in Coventry, subsequently purchased by the Armstrong Siddeley Owners Club. (ASHT)

Road to spend their evenings moving trays of parts from racks. Then racks and trays would all be taken to the new stores. Sleep must have been a rare commodity. The ASOC took over the worldwide supply of Armstrong Siddeley car parts to customers, whether club members or not. To regularise this new activity the club was registered as a limited company and all its members became shareholders. This is still the situation today, nearly half a century later.

The spare parts premises are known as the stores and still contain a sizeable quantity of those original new parts. Naturally over time some of them, particularly those incorporating the use of rubber, have become unserviceable and have been scrapped, but many of the parts are still perfectly useable. Lots of the parts with a high turnover have long since sold out but have been replaced with brand-new parts remanufactured to at least original specification. In addition the club has stepped in to buy stocks of parts, new and second-hand, wherever possible to ensure the continuity of parts availability. Parts availability for pre-war cars is limited, although still better than for the majority of cars of a similar age from other makers. Tucked away in one or two corners are parts from ancient cars that may be beyond refurbishment but could still act as useful patterns. Post-war cars are well served, particularly for mechanical parts. Although some new panels are still held, the choice is more likely to be restricted to used panels. It is impossible to keep every part in stock; for example the post-war 16/18 hp cars used at least three slightly different front wings while in production. New parts remanufactured are mostly those needed to keep cars roadworthy but some body parts like bumpers have also been made in small batches when there is sufficient demand to keep prices affordable. Prices are reasonable for such rare parts, but then this has to be the case as club members are also shareholders and so they have a large say in the actions of the unpaid volunteer company directors. Profits from the sales of spare parts are put back into buying new parts.

The continuing supply of spare parts is remarkable when one considers that Armstrong Siddeley Motors was in business for forty-one years between 1919 and 1960, while the club has been existence for even longer from 1960 to date, and spare parts have been available since 1919. The bold move taken by the club when it started to supply spare parts has enabled many cars that would have otherwise been long since scrapped to stay on the road.

Apart from its spare parts operations the ASOC provides all members with the usual club benefits. The monthly colour magazine *Sphinx* has reports of social activities, maintenance and restoration advice and cars for sale. *Sphinx* is backed up by the club website, www.siddeley.org, which is open to all and has a section accessible to members only. Regular local meetings and events, an annual static rally and occasional international events are organised for members. The club takes pride in the social side of membership and is equally popular with member's partners, who enjoy getting together without the necessity of listening to technical chatter.

For those members labouring over repairs or restorations alone in their garage and finding a difficult problem the club has a network of experts, listed in the club magazine, who are willing to dispense the benefits of their knowledge and experience over the phone.

Overseas Armstrong Siddeley enthusiasts are also well looked after by active clubs in Australia, New Zealand, the Netherlands and Germany.

With a membership numbering around 800 and many members renewing their membership for many years, the club must be doing some things right.

While the clubs are dedicated to keeping Armstrong Siddeleys on the road and to providing an active social life for their members, there is a sister organisation devoted to preserving the heritage of the marque. The Armstrong Siddeley Heritage Trust exists to preserve the history of the marque and allied companies that were part of Lord Kenilworth's empire. The trust has been registered as a charity because this ensures a high degree of long-term security for its growing collection of artefacts. Membership is open to all but the majority of members are also club members.

The original idea behind the trust was to try to save those many gems of historical importance that Armstrong Siddeley enthusiasts often collect but are then lost forever after their death when executors, unaware of what they are dealing with, often consign such items to a tip or a bonfire. From a small start the trust has now built up to more proactive actions than were originally envisaged. Working in conjunction with English Heritage, a long-term exhibition about John Siddeley, the first Lord Kenilworth, has been established in the gatehouse at Kenilworth Castle – a particular appropriate place to celebrate John Siddeley's life as he purchased the castle and gave it to the nation.

This partially restored Hurricane was owned from new by Sir Malcolm Campbell of land speed record fame, although not in this car. It has been acquired by the Armstrong Siddeley Owners Club, which is continuing the restoration.

A large collection of original factory negatives that were discarded when car production ceased have been purchased by the Trust and are gradually being digitised to preserve them, as many of the negatives have started to deteriorate due to poor storage. They are now kept in a low-humidity and low-temperature storage environment to halt the deterioration as far as possible. The slow and painstaking work of digitising these pictures is revealing unknown or forgotten aspects of Armstrong Siddeley history. Sadly, a large part of the original company archive was lost during air raids on Coventry, which makes the surviving pictures all the more important.

The Trust is fortunate to have been the recipient of three complete Armstrong Siddeley cars. A very fine 1935 17 hp car that is taken to a number of events each year to publicise the Trust attracts a good deal of attention wherever it goes. In one respect it is thought to be unique as it was fitted with special modifications (still in situ) for a disabled driver in 1952. The company that fitted them says that it is the earliest car recorded with these controls. A 14 hp car was passed to the Armstrong Siddeley Heritage Trust by the Rolls-Royce Heritage Trust when it lost some storage space. After a little light work to prepare the car for exhibition it has been passed to the Armstrong family in Bamburgh Castle, where it is displayed in the Armstrong and Aviation Artefacts Museum.

A third car in the care of the trust is a Sapphire 346, sadly currently in poor condition and needing restoration attention when funds permit. Under normal circumstances the cost would be difficult to justify but this car has an interesting history as it was used as a guinea pig when the criteria for the first MOT tests were being established. It would undoubtedly fail an MOT test at the moment, but when restored it will become another way to promote the Trust and will be a proud example of the work of the Parkside factory in Coventry.

Aside from these major items, the Trust has been gifted or has acquired many artefacts of all sizes, all of which are a part of the company history and many of which have an interesting tale to tell. Other parts of the ever-growing collection form a useful reference resource.

The Trust also issues a twice-yearly journal, *Siddeley Times*, which relates many previously unrecounted aspects of Armstrong Siddeley heritage interest, as well as news

These sphinx mascots are part of the J. D. Siddeley exhibition at Kenilworth Castle. The sphinx at the front right is from a Sapphire 346 and shows its winglets with suspended Sapphire jet engines.

of the trust's activities. More information about the trust can be found on its website www.armstrongsiddeleyheritagetrust.com. In addition, the Rolls-Royce Heritage Trust is an organisation that specialises in preserving the aviation history of Rolls-Royce and Armstrong Siddeley.

The Armstrong Siddeley Heritage Trust's 17 hp Burlington-bodied D back saloon.

This painting of a Hurricane, by the well-known artist Frank Wootton, was used in advertising the car. It is one of a pair of Wootton paintings that were generously donated to the Armstrong Siddeley Heritage Trust. The other painting, which shows a Whitley, adorns the cover of this book. (ASHT)

Bibliography

Bastow, Donald, *W. O. Bentley – Engineer* (G. T. Foulis and Co., 1978).

Bentley, Walter Owen, *My Life and My Cars* (New Jersey, USA, American edition: A. S. Barnes & Co. Inc., 1969).

Betts, Alan, *Stoneleigh Motors, An Armstrong Siddeley* Company (Derby: Rolls-Royce Heritage Trust, 2006).

Bradly, Robert Penn, *Armstrong Siddeley – The Postwar Cars* (Croydon: Motor Racing Publications Ltd, 1989).

Bradly, Robert Penn, *Armstrong Siddeley Cars – The Complete Collection* (New South Wales, Australia: Limula Pty Ltd, 2014).

Bramson, Alan, *Pure Luck* (Yeovil: Patrick Stephens Ltd/Haynes Publishing Group plc, 1990).

Brendon, Piers, *The Motoring Century: The Story of the RAC* (London: Bloomsbury Publishing, 1997).

Clausager, Anders Ditlev, *Wolseley, A Very British Car* (Beaworthy: Herridge & Sons Ltd, 2016).

Cook, Ray, *Armstrong Siddeley: The Parkside Story 1896–1939* (Derby: Rolls-Royce Heritage Trust, 1988).

Couper, Mike, *Rallying to Monte Carlo* (London: Sportsmans Book Club edition, 1957).

Cowbourne, Donals, *British Trial Drivers, Their Cars and Awards 1902–1914* (Otley: Westbury Publishing, 2003).

Harper, Martin, *Mr Lionel* (London: Cassell & Co. Ltd, 1970).

Lawton, Roy, *Parkside – Armstrong Siddeley to Rolls-Royce 1939–1994* (Derby: The Rolls-Royce Heritage Trust, 2008).

Lord Montagu, *The Gordon Bennett Races* (London: Motor Races Book Club, first published by Cassell & Co. Ltd 1963).

Sharp, Selwyn (editor), *The Evening and the Morning* (Coventry: Armstrong Siddeley Motors Ltd, 1957).

Smith, Bill, *Armstrong Siddeley Motors* (Dorchester: Veloce Publishing Ltd, 2006).

William, David E., *A View of Ansty 1935–1982* (Derby: Rolls-Royce Heritage Trust, 1998).

Wilson, Gordon A., *Walter Wilson, Portrait of An Inventor* (London: Gerald Duckworth & Co. Ltd, 1986).

Additional information was sourced from:

Grace's Guide to British Industrial History (www.gracesguide.co.uk).

Various issues of *Autosport* and *The Motor*, courtesy of Vintage Sports Car Club archive.

Various issues of *Employees' Quarterly*, courtesy of Rolls-Royce Heritage Trust.

Original Siddeley Deasy and Armstrong Siddeley documents, courtesy of the Herbert Gallery in Coventry.

Various issues of *The Hawker Siddeley Review*, the Armstrong Siddeley Owners Club magazine *Sphinx*, and the Armstrong Siddeley Heritage Trust journal *Siddeley Times* in the author's collection.

Acknowledgements

I am indebted to many friends in the Armstrong Siddeley Owners Club and in the Armstrong Siddeley Heritage Trust for their help and support in writing this book and in giving me access to many pictures.

Every attempt has been made to seek permission for copyright material used in this book. However, if we have inadvertently used copyright material without permission/acknowledgement we apologise and we will make the necessary correction at the first opportunity.

Particular thanks to Chris Allen and Iain Campbell for proofreading the script of this book. Iain has also devoted many hours to searching the Armstrong Siddeley Heritage Trust archive for pictures that have not seen the light of day for generations. Thanks also to my sister, Ann Blatchford, for looking up many car details on the Armstrong Siddeley Owners Club database. I would also like to thank Connor Stait and his colleagues at Amberley Publishing for their help and guidance in producing this book.

The Herbert Gallery in Coventry has also been very kind in searching out documents from their archives for me to consult. Many people have helped me during the writing of this book – friends, and some who were total strangers before I contacted them, have helped in innumerable ways, and I thank them all. Any mistakes that remain are my responsibility.

If it is not too pretentious to dedicate such a small book as this then I dedicate it firstly to John Davenport Siddeley and the staff of Armstrong Siddeley Motors, whose cars have given me great joy since my childhood, and secondly to my great nephew, Arthur Blatchford, who is currently a toddler, in the hope that one day he too will share the fun of driving an Armstrong Siddeley – one of life's great pleasures.